THE

Young Adult's Survival Guide to Interviews

Finding the Job and Nailing the Interview

Rebekah Sack

The Young Adult's Survival Guide to Interviews:
Finding the Job and Nailing the Interview

Library of Congress Cataloging-in-Publication Data

Names: Bennick, Rebekah, 1994- author.
Title: The young adult's survival guide to interviews : finding the job and
    nailing the interview / Rebekah Bennick.
Description: Ocala, Florida : Atlantic Pub. Group, Inc., [2016] | Includes
    bibliographical references and index.
Identifiers: LCCN 2016010360 (print) | LCCN 2016015449 (ebook) | ISBN
    9781601389909 (alk. paper) | ISBN 1601389906 (alk. paper) | ISBN
    9781620230015 ()
Subjects: LCSH: Employment interviewing--Juvenile literature. | Job
    hunting--Juvenile literature.
Classification: LCC HF5549.5.I6 B445 2016 (print) | LCC HF5549.5.I6 (ebook) |
    DDC 650.14/4--dc23
LC record available at https://lccn.loc.gov/2016010360

Reduce. Reuse. RECYCLE.

A decade ago, Atlantic Publishing signed the Green Press Initiative. These guidelines promote environmentally friendly practices, such as using recycled stock and vegetable-based inks, avoiding waste, choosing energy-efficient resources, and promoting a no-pulping policy. We now use 100-percent recycled stock on all our books. The results: in one year, switching to post-consumer recycled stock saved 24 mature trees, 5,000 gallons of water, the equivalent of the total energy used for one home in a year, and the equivalent of the greenhouse gases from one car driven for a year.

Over the years, we have adopted a number of dogs from rescues and shelters. First there was Bear and after he passed, Ginger and Scout. Now, we have Kira, another rescue. They have brought immense joy and love into not just into our lives, but into the lives of all who met them.

We want you to know a portion of the profits of this book will be donated in Bear, Ginger and Scout's memory to local animal shelters, parks, conservation organizations, and other individuals and nonprofit organizations in need of assistance.

— **Douglas & Sherri Brown,**
President & Vice-President of Atlantic Publishing

TABLE OF CONTENTS

INTRODUCTION

What comes to mind when you think about the word "interview"?

Do you see yourself sitting in a cold, metal chair (in a dark room, naturally) with a spotlight on your face?

Do you see a close-up of your forehead, a bead of sweat forming against your hairline, and those annoying little baby hairs frizzing up or your socks becoming soaked like they always do during gym class?

Can you feel your armpits heating up, your hands dampening, your legs trembling and your mouth drying up?

You are not alone in this. A recent study by Harris Interactive found that 92 percent of adults in the United States have anxiety about job interviews. And that's adults — they're supposed to be the calm ones, right?

There is a biological reason that we get nervous for job interviews. You aren't abnormal or strange; it is in your blood. According to Dr. Tamar Chansky, author of *Freeing Yourself From Anxiety*, interviewing can feel a lot like getting attacked by a wild animal. He explains, "When we perceive that we are in a high stakes situation, the brain doesn't distinguish the high stakes of a job interview — where it would help to be calm, cool and collected — from the high stakes of being under threat from attack (say, from a tiger)."

Basically, you can blame your intense nervousness on your brain.

While you won't be able to get rid of every nervous cell in your body, you can get rid of most of them by understanding what is going to happen and by preparing yourself.

This book is going to explain everything you need to know about interviewing, from finding the job you want to following up afterward.

Let's get started.

CHAPTER ONE

Finding the Job

The first thing you need to do to prepare yourself for an interview is to find the job. To find the job, you need to know what job would be the best one for you.

What Job Suits You?

So, we know this isn't going to be your career. You probably won't be doing this for the rest of your life, but you should still find a job that you won't be dreading every day. The best way to do this is to find a job that fits well with who you are.

Think about your personality — what traits would you say describe you the best? Are you shy (introverted) or outgoing (extroverted)? To determine this, think about what you would prefer to do. If prefer reading a book to going to a slumber party, you're probably introverted.

Are you full of energy or do you prefer to lay low? In other words, are you the one playing on the basketball team or the one sitting on the sidelines?

Do you like doing things for others? I know what you're thinking — the answer is a huge, whopping "no" (of course I don't like doing the dishes and vacuuming the living room) — but many jobs out there are for people with a nurturing personality. Think about jobs like being a nurse or a teacher.

Can you handle stress well? When it's the end of the semester and you have four exams to study for, are you freaking out or are you confident?

These kinds of questions will help you when you're thinking about what kind of job will be the best one for you. Let's dig a little deeper.

Are you shy?

If you determined that you tend to fall on the shy side, the kinds of jobs you are going to be best at are jobs where you don't have to interact with other people.

Some examples of jobs like this where you're working behind the scenes include the following:

- Working at a movie theatre, perhaps as an usher
- Working at a restaurant as a cook or a busboy
- Working with animals; this includes animal shelters, pet stores, or zoos
- Working at a library shelving material
- Working at a car wash

- Working at a grocery store; there are a lot of positions in a grocery store that don't require interaction with people (think stocking shelves or working in the meat department)
- Working at a warehouse; this includes loading and unloading inventory (you should consider the size of your muscles before applying for this job)
- Working on a farm; depending on where you live, you may find that farmers need help
- Working as a lifeguard
- Doing paper delivery

These are just a few examples of jobs that would mesh well with your shy side.

However, just because you are shy doesn't mean that you are unable to work with customers. Consider stepping out of your comfort zone — maybe you aren't as shy as you thought you were. This would be the perfect time to find out.

Are you outgoing?

If your friends refer to you as "the loud one," you're probably an extrovert. Any job that allows for interaction with people is probably going to be a good one for you.

Some examples of jobs like this include:

- Working in retail; working for any kind of retail store including clothing stores, supermarkets, or malls
- Working at a restaurant as a cashier or a server
- Working at a grocery store as a cashier or a bagger
- Doing pizza delivery

- Working anywhere as a receptionist (you are most likely to find this kind of job in the medical field; think dentist, doctor, chiropractor, eye doctor)

This list looks shorter than the shy one, but these categories are much larger. Think about all of the stores in your city — every single store needs people that are interacting with customers. Consider the stores that align with your interests and go from there.

Are you a great communicator?

If you're really great at communicating, consider being a server. One of a server's main jobs is to communicate with customers and the rest of the staff. Servers should be able to communicate with a wide range of personalities.

If your friends often tell you that you're good at "reading people," then being a server would be a great fit. Part of the job is being able to read people's facial and body expressions. For example: You will need to feel out whether a guest is interested in chatting or not. If a solitary customer is reading, the server shouldn't hang around just because he or she assumes the guest is lonely. If the guest encourages conversation, that's fine; otherwise, the guest may simply be interested in the book he or she has brought along.

Do you have a lot of energy?

Think about jobs that require you to be constantly moving. This includes serving, working any kind of physical labor job (farming, construction, that warehouse job), or being a paperboy.

If you find yourself wanting to take a nap at two in the afternoon, consider doing a job that doesn't require you to be high-energy at all times.

Can you handle stress well?

The restaurant world is a stressful one, and servers will have to deal with physical and mental stress on a daily basis. This stress can take the form of annoying customers, a sassy kitchen crew, another server that won't pull his or her own weight, or simply dealing with a busy restaurant.

Any business that is thriving will have a certain level of stress attached to it. A busy business is constantly moving, and you will need to be able to keep up.

Do you have a desire to please others?

Are you the kind of person that prefers giving gifts rather than receiving them?

If this sounds like you, it means you like pleasing others. Working in retail or the restaurant industry will be a great fit for you. Any industry that allows a customer to tip you for a superior service will be a good fit — your desire to please others will actually make you more money.

Do you like children?

If you like children, babysitting might be the perfect job for you. Oftentimes, parents only need babysitters Friday and Saturday nights. This leaves the majority of your week open for schoolwork and other commitments. If you find yourself very busy with school, and yet still want some sort of job, this is a perfect option for you.

Where to Look

Now that you have an idea of what kind of job you want to apply for, you need to find one that's actually hiring. There are four main ways to go about finding a job: using social media, the local newspaper, going door-to-door, looking at Craigslist and utilizing family connections.

Social media

This is a great first place to start when looking for a job. The first thing you can do is to create a post asking about hiring businesses: "Hello Facebook friends! I am on the job hunt — does anyone know of any businesses that are hiring right now?"

You are bound to receive some responses. The great part about this kind of resource is that you can use the name of the person that gave you the suggestion. For example: "I am looking for a job and heard about your business through *name of person*. Are you currently hiring?"

This gives you some ethos. Ethos is the appeal to ethics; it is a means of convincing someone else that you have great character and are a credible person.

The other option you have with social media is to look for special pages. There are Facebook pages that cater to certain cities or areas. For example: **For Sale in Orlando** or **For Rent in Miami**.

Do a search for jobs in your area. Use search terms such as "**Hiring in My City**" or "**Job Openings in My City**." People are constantly posting to pages such as this; there is a chance that a job will be posted that will interest you.

Local newspaper

Because the Internet is taking the world by storm, it should be the first place you look. However, the local newspaper is a great Plan B.

There is often a "Help Wanted" section in the newspaper, and you know it's real people posting these ads, not spammers (spammers aren't going to pay for a spot in the paper).

Consider browsing the section; you never know what you might find.

Door-to-door

This method may sound outdated or foreign to you, but don't discount the power of going door-to-door.

Do you ever see signs that say "We're Hiring"? Businesses often post these signs on their doors — keep an eye out for signs like this when you're on the job hunt.

Even if a sign isn't on the door, that doesn't necessarily mean that the business isn't hiring.

Visit several businesses. Build up your courage and ask for a manager. Ask if they're hiring; if the answer is "yes" or "no, but we are accepting applications," ask for an application.

Many businesses do all of their application process online; you may just get a website name. However, introducing yourself to the manager is the first step to being memorable. Be sure to introduce yourself by name twice. Once at the beginning — "Hi, my name is *X*." — and once at the end — "Thank you very much. Again, my name is *X*."

Studies show that the average human needs to hear something seven times before they actually remember it. Saying your name seven times might earn you an eyebrow raise or a weird look, so saying it twice is about the best you can do.

Family connections

Not everyone will have this as an option. Maybe your parents aren't involved in the community or you're new in town. However, if you do have this option, use it!

Ask your parents to ask around; you are more likely to get a job if you have some kind of connection to the person that is hiring. Many professionals will tell you that they got a lot of their jobs through some kind of connection — this is also referred to as *networking*. According to a study done by ABC News in 2012, about 80 percent of jobs are had through networking. If you have this option, use it.

Craigslist

Craigslist is not the first place you should go when looking for a job. In fact, it should really be your last resort.

The reason for this is that Craigslist is full of spam — there are a lot of fake posts made by either creepy people or robots. Sometimes it's obvious that the post is fake, but other times it isn't. If you do decide to try out Craigslist, be cautious.

If you go to the website for your particular city, you will see an entire list under the heading "Jobs." Within this section there will be a variety of subsections with titles like "admin," "customer service," or "food."

Browse through all of the headings that sound interesting to you. Obviously, you will not be able to apply for all of the jobs listed

— you can't exactly work in real estate yet — so be realistic with your expectations.

If you find one that sounds like a winner, send an email. Be wary of the response and don't give out any personal information (your address or financial information, especially).

Age Requirements

Depending on your age, there are some restrictions about what kinds of jobs you can hold and how long you can work. These restrictions range based on where you live. For example, if you live in Illinois, you can start working as young as 10, while in Ohio, you have to be at least 14.

To see a full list of these requirements, you can visit the United States Department of Labor website (**www.dol.gov**).

Below is some general, federal information on what you can do at what age. All of the following information is taken from the U.S. Department of Labor website as well as Youth Rules!, a government website for teens (**www.youthrules.gov**). Find your age and read on.

Under 14

If you are under 14, there are still some jobs you can do. These include:

- Delivering newspapers
- Babysitting
- Working as an actor or performer

- Working as a homeworker gathering evergreens and making evergreen wreaths (We aren't making this up; this is actually a thing)
- Working for a business owned entirely by your parents as long as it doesn't fall into the hazardous job category

If any of these interest you, you're good to go. If you're interested in agriculture, you're going to have to look at the rules for your particular state.

14 or 15

If you are 14 or 15, you have more options as to what you can do, but you're still limited on how many hours you can work (is that so bad?).

Here are some guidelines on how much you can work:

- No more than three hours on a school day, including Friday
- No more than 18 hours per week when school is in session
- No more than eight hours per day when school is not in session
- No more than 40 hours per week when school is not in session
- No working before 7 a.m. or after 7 p.m. on any day, except from June 1st through Labor Day, when nighttime work hours are extended to 9 p.m.

Now that you know how much you can work, take a look at the kinds of jobs you can do:

- Anything in retail (we're looking at you, extrovert)

- Anything intellectual or creative such as computer programming, teaching, tutoring, singing, acting, or playing an instrument
- Errands or delivery work by foot, bicycle and public transportation
- General yard work
- Doing work on cars (things like car washing and polishing)
- Some kitchen and food service work
- Loading or unloading objects for use at a worksite
- If you meet the requirements, you can perform limited tasks in sawmills and woodshops
- If you meet the requirements, you can be a lifeguard

16 or 17

If you're 16 or 17, you're pretty much able to do anything, with just a few restrictions.

You can work as much as you want (blessing or curse?), and you can work any job you want, as long as it isn't declared as one of the "hazardous" jobs — you know, working with explosives and stuff.

18 and above

You are as free as a bird. You can do whatever you want and as much as you want to do it.

Those hazardous jobs are all fair game — if you ever wanted to be a coal miner or that guy that stops forest fires, it's all up for grabs.

How to get a work permit

The federal government doesn't require you to have a work permit. However, the rules change depending on what state you live in.

To find out if you need a work permit for being underage, visit this website **www.dol.gov/whd/state/certification.htm**. This site has a table with every state; find yours to see if you need a permit.

If you find out that you do need a permit, here's what you need to do.

Let's use Illinois as an example. On the table, you can see that if you are under 16, you need a work permit. You will also see that the table tells you where to get that work permit from — the labor department or your school. This will vary depending on what state you're in. For Illinois, you need it from your school.

If you need it from your school, all you have to do is ask the superintendent. They'll know what to do.

If you need it from the labor department, you'll have to go to the town hall. They have the form there — you'll just have to fill it out.

It's pretty simple. The permit will ask to fill out general information like your name and address and where you go to school. Once you have all of it filled out, you should be ready to get to work.

CHAPTER TWO

Preparing for the Interview

So, you've found the job you want to apply for. At this point, you need to prepare for a possible interview. To do that, you need to research the company, understand the different interview formats, and know how to present yourself.

Research the Company

Nothing looks worse to your future boss than being unprepared. All companies have a history, and it will help you to know a little bit about it. Most companies have a website, so all you have to do is go to the "About Us" section.

Pay special attention to the mission statement; this is going to be the basic principal of the company — it's basically what they stand for. For example, the mission statement of Wal-Mart[SM] centers on helping people live better by saving them money. Their slogan is "Save Money. Live Better," and they're also known for the phrase "Every day low

prices." If you go to their website, they have a "Get to Know Us" section, and that is where you will find this kind of information.

Also try to remember key names and dates. For example, try to remember the names of the founders of the company or the year that the company started. Even if you could care less, try your best to show genuine interest in the history of the company — after all, you may become part of it.

If you do this kind of research, it will show in your interview. There is no doubt that your future boss will be impressed that you took the time (don't tell her it only took two minutes) to research their company. Not only will you be showing off your smarts, you'll be avoiding a possible embarrassing moment if you're asked a question about the company and you don't know the answer (hot pink cheeks avoided).

Types of Interviews

The interview process can take different forms. For your first job, you are most likely to encounter a phone interview, a one-on-one interview, or a group interview. It's also possible that you will have multiple interviews and in different forms. You'll probably get a phone call from the employer asking you to come in for a one-on-one interview — this is generally the standard. You need to be prepared for the phone call, as your future boss might slip in a mini interview before you actually get to the real thing.

Phone interview

A phone interview is usually the first interview. Regardless of the reason for the interview, the goal is the same — you're trying to get a face-to-face interview. In this case, you're going to want to have your research done before you actually get the phone call, which means you need to be completely prepared when you send in your application.

Since a phone interview restricts communication to only sound, you have to do a lot more work when it comes to paying attention to your voice. (The plus side being that you can be wearing pajamas with cucumbers on your eyes for all they know.)

Tone of voice is a very intricate thing, and we will go into much more detail in Chapter 4, but just be aware that the way you are talking is all your future boss has to go off of. In other words, they are judging you by the sound of your voice.

Some things to remember when it comes to phone interviews are:

- Be enthusiastic (but not obnoxiously fake about it)
- Stay focused
- Do not be doing anything else at the same time; your distraction will be noticed
- Turn off any background music
- Remove yourself from your family (a piece of advice you'll probably never see again)
- Turn off any distractions
- Take notes
- Remember to ask questions
- Consider practicing phone interviews with a friend
- Don't be eating or chewing gum during the phone call
- Don't ask about how much you'll be paid over the phone (odds are it's going to be minimum wage)
- Speak slowly and clearly (but not too slowly or too clearly — you don't want it look like you're undermining their intelligence)

One-on-one interviews

This is the most common type of interview. This is you talking to one person — this is that image from the beginning of the book of you sitting in a dark, metal chair with a spotlight on your face.

The person interviewing you will ask you some questions, some easy ones and some challenging ones. Their goal is to have an idea of who you are and whether or not you would be a good person for the job.

The interview starts when you shake hands with the interviewer. In this first few minutes, he or she will have already read various signals from you that you may not even think about. This includes your body language (what you're doing with your hands, how fast or slow your walking pace is) other non-verbal signals (your facial expression, even down to how your eyebrows look — is one raised? can you even raise one eyebrow?), and the way you are dressed.

Be conscious about what you're doing with your body. Think about how you're coming across. This first impression is everything.

Group interview

In a group interview, there is more than one person applying for the same position and everyone is doing the interview at the same time.

With this type of interview, the company is looking to see:

- Who are the leaders
- Stress levels of each candidate
- How the candidate faces the situation

- Communication skills in a group setting
- The knowledge level of each person

This type of interview can make it difficult to get equal time while giving the other people a chance to speak. Ignore others that are being aggressive or difficult. This is not usually a final interview. It is often a way to get through many candidates to find those to be short-listed (which is a good thing; it means you passed the first interview).

What to Wear

What you should wear to an interview is highly dependent on where you are interviewing. As a general rule of thumb, for most first jobs, business casual is the way to go. While business casual is a pretty ambiguous term, it falls on a spectrum.

The spectrum looks like this:

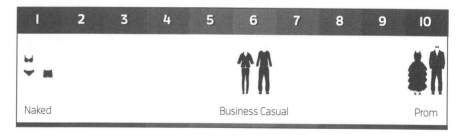

Business casual falls at about a 6. The phrase generally refers to clothing that is pretty casual but very neat and professional looking. Think golf clothes — khakis or slacks and a polo shirt. For women, this might mean dress pants or a knee-length skirt and a button down shirt or a nice blouse. Make sure your dress shirt is ironed. Wearing an outfit that

looks like you just picked it up out of your dirty clothes bin is never impressive.

A tuxedo or a suit (probably a 9 on the scale) will probably be a little too much for your first job interview. Your employer might be very impressed with how serious you're taking the job, but in the end, they'll think you look a little silly and overdressed.

The same goes for the other side of the scale. Showing up in pajamas (a 1.5) or a t-shirt and shorts (a 3.5) won't impress anyone. Even if the job is casual and the workers are wearing super casual clothing, the interview is a more formal event — you're expected to dress up a little bit.

If you're interviewing for a clothing store, don't show up with a competitor's logo branded on your polo. It will draw negative attention to you and your boss will be turned off.

Dealing with Anxiety

Anxiety is the most common mental health problem in the United States. In fact, according to Chris Lewis, Ed.S., it affects over 90 percent of us at least once (2013). You're totally normal. Being nervous is part of life — it's actually a good thing. If we never got nervous, we'd take more risks, putting us in danger. Your interviewer will actually think it's *good* that you're nervous. It means that you care.

However, if you feel like your anxiety is stopping you in any way, don't think that you have to go running to the doc for meds. There are a lot of simple things you can do that can help reduce your anxiety. Some of them might make you laugh because they're so strange (I should start laughing? seriously?), but they really do help.

Belly breathing

Lewis gives a lot of good examples in his article "High Anxiety: Three Simple Ways to Calm Your Nerves." One of the things he talks about is belly breathing. When we're nervous, sometimes we can make ourselves more nervous just by breathing wrong.

When your mom told you to take deep breaths, she wasn't kidding — it actually sends a signal to your brain, telling it that everything is okay. Your brain starts kicking out stress hormones and your heart rate slows down. Before you know it, your anxiety is going away!

To do this, Lewis tells you to put a hand on your stomach and a hand on your chest. Start breathing really deeply. Your goal is to have the hand on your stomach rising up and down, not the one on your chest. Try it now — see how when you breathe really deeply, your stomach starts to rise? It's a really easy way to help you calm down when you feel like a panic attack is coming.

Take a walk

Studies show that exercise helps to calm nerves. You're taking away all your physical tension when you exercise. Before your interview, take a walk around the block. Feeling extra nervous? Go jogging.

You'll be amazed at how much better you'll feel once you've released some endorphins (the feel-good hormone in your brain).

Journal

Keeping a journal may seem a little dramatic (Dear Diary?), but studies show that writing down your thoughts and anxieties helps release them from your brain. Your brain is so worried that it will forget the important stuff that it actually makes you more anxious. When you write it down, your brains stops worrying about forgetting.

Laugh

When you laugh, you're tricking your brain into thinking it's calm and relaxed. This is similar to how smiling can trick your brain into thinking it's happy. Do both right before you walk in to your interview. It may seem silly — am I really sitting in my car laughing right now? — but try it next time you're nervous. You'll be glad you did.

CHAPTER THREE

Sample Questions for Beginners

You know some facts about the company, you know what to expect when it comes to the different types of interviewing, you have your outfit picked out, and you're working on calming your nerves. The next step is knowing what kinds of questions you will be asked.

The beginning of the interview will consist of common, simple questions that involve getting to know you and where you are in life.

These are the kinds of questions that you probably know the answers to right off the top of your head, but be sure to browse through them in case there's one that you don't know.

Getting to Know You

Your boss wants to get a sense of who you are. These questions are centered on your interests and hobbies.

- What is the hobby or activity you have participated in the longest?
- What are the first three things you do when you get up in the morning?
- What activities do you do in your spare time?

ANALYSIS: The answers to these questions will give the interviewer a glimpse at what you value. For instance, if you want to showcase your education, the answers you give should emphasize academic performance or activity. You may describe yourself in terms of your favorite subject and education goals, or your greatest accomplishment may be a scholastic achievement.

Be honest. Don't think too hard about the answers to these — if you have always loved singing, and it's the first thing that comes to mind, just say it. Your interviewer wants to get to know who you are; if you lie or say something that doesn't really represent you, you aren't letting them in.

If you can't think of anything, or feel like you don't have any special hobbies, think about what you do when you get home from school. What is the first thing that you're most excited about? If it's playing video games, say you're interested in gaming. If it's watching television, say you're interested in film. Often times, just using more sophisticated wording will make you seem more professional and put-together.

Work History

These kinds of questions are used to understand your experience level.

- Can you give me a brief summary of your work history up to this point?
- What have you accomplished in the past that makes you particularly qualified for this position?

ANALYSIS: If you haven't had any jobs before, it's okay. You are applying for an entry-level position; you aren't necessarily expected to have too much of a work history.

Try to think of something that you've done that has helped you qualify for the position you're applying for. For example, if you're applying for a position as a cashier, now is the time to tell your future boss that you're great at math or that you're the class secretary.

Why This Job?

Make sure you choose a job that you're actually interested in, because these kinds of questions may come up.

- Why did you apply for this job?
- How did you hear about this job opening?
- What have you done to prepare for this interview?
- What motivated you to be interested in this position?

ANALYSIS: The way you answer these types of questions is important. They may help to separate you from other candidates with similar qualifications. Often, the person who wants the position more will put in the extra time and energy necessary to be successful.

These kinds of questions also make it clear that you need to apply for a company that you are interested in. That way, you can say, "Because I love your food," "The clothes here are my favorite," or "Because I love film."

The fact that you're reading this book is a great answer to the preparation question. Also, now is the time to tell your boss that you researched the company's history (brownie points won).

School-Related Questions

These kinds of questions are also about getting to know you, but they are framed around your schooling.

- What school do you go to?
- What grade are you in?
- What is your favorite subject in school?
- What is your best subject in school?
- If you plan on going to college, do you know what you would like to major in?
- What course gave you the most difficulty?

ANALYSIS: If you don't have any work experience, use these questions to share information about your strengths. Being a student is like having a job — in fact, many companies, including the government, offer it as an option when they ask you what your occupation is.

Although work is different than school, it still requires you to have the following traits: communication, teamwork, motivation, initiative and organization. If one of these is your strong suit, now is the time to highlight it.

When you're asked questions that force you to talk about your weaknesses (what subject is your worst one?), be honest. The worst possible answer to this question is "I don't have a worst subject" or "I'm good at all of them."

We are all human, and we all have weaknesses; your interviewer knows this. Your employer is trying to find out if your weakness will hinder you from being able to do the job you are applying for. The best way to answer this question is to reframe it. For example, "I had the most trouble with history, because I find that I'm not as interested in it as I am in English."

This way, you're softening the blow by providing a positive response.

CHAPTER FOUR

Sample Questions for Experts

Once the beginning questions are over, the interview will then progress into harder to answer questions that might leave you speechless (ever had a moment where you just didn't know what to say?). Don't freak out just yet — take a little time to browse through these questions as well as the analysis of them.

Simply knowing what's coming can calm your nerves more than you might think (clammy hands be gone!).

Most of these questions are going to ask you to talk about a specific situation you've been in. This is where the practicing and preparation comes in. You need to actually think of those situations. Other questions will ask you about your personality and character traits. You need to think about who you are and what defines you to answer them well.

Job Performance

These questions target your strengths and weaknesses when it comes to your job performance.

- What kind of supervision do you think brings out the best in you?
- Do you prefer to work alone or as a part of a group?
- What are some job responsibilities you do not like?

ANALYSIS: These kinds of questions get you in the habit of thinking about a job in particular rather than work in general. Consider your personality and your experience in school when answering these questions.

Did you produce your best work when you had a strict teacher or a lenient one?

Do you love group projects or do you hate them?

Self-Evaluation

These kinds of questions force you to think about who you are as a person. You're young — no one expects you to fully know who you are yet. However, you should have a general idea of your ethics.

Ethics are your moral compass. When you're in a situation where you are forced to choose between right and wrong, you are using your ethics. Ethics are often connected to religious beliefs. For example, in Buddhism, the ethical principals include no killing, stealing, or lying.

Ethics can seem pretty black and white (of course I shouldn't kill anyone...) but there is a gray area.

For example, let's say that your friend says to you, "Did you know that Cody is cheating on his girlfriend?"

Do you think it is your ethical responsibility to relay this information to Cody's girlfriend? On the one hand, it really isn't any of your business. But on the other hand, you would be giving her very valuable information that exposes some truth in her life, which will ultimately be helping her a great deal.

What do you do? Your answer to this kind of question determines who you are. Your employer probably won't ask you about Cody, but he may ask you some questions like these:

- As an employee, how do you describe yourself?
- How would your last supervisor describe you?
- How would your co-workers describe you?
- What type of job-related activity are you most confident performing?
- What has given you the most satisfaction at work?
- How do you know when you have done a good job?
- On a scale from 1-10, how detail-oriented are you?

ANALYSIS: The primary purpose of self-evaluation questions is for the interviewer to uncover which characteristics you find the most valuable. Whatever qualities you focus on should be the ones that you believe are the most important to the position for which you are applying.

Some examples of describing qualities are:

- Accountability: Can people count on you? Are you responsible for your own actions?
- Chivalry: Do you open doors for people? Are you generally kind?
- Commitment: Are you dedicated to things for long periods of time?
- Compassion: Are you sympathetic towards other people who may be less fortunate or who are suffering?
- Confidence: Do you believe in yourself and your abilities?
- Courage: Do you do things that frighten you?
- Creativity: Are you constantly coming up with new ideas?
- Decisiveness: When your mom asks you where you want to go for dinner, do you answer with a decisive suggestion or "I don't care"?
- Enthusiasm: Are you eager, interested and excited about things?
- Flexibility: Are you willing to adapt to new things?
- Generosity: Are you kind and willing to give things away?
- Goal-oriented: Are you motivated to reach a specific goal?
- Honesty: When your mom asks who took the cookie from the cookie jar, how do you respond?
- Initiative: Do you take charge before other people do?
- Integrity: Do you have strong moral principles? Are you honest?
- Kindness: Are you a friendly person?
- Leadership: Are you usually the one that takes over in the group project? Are you the team captain?
- Loyalty: Are you capable of being devoted to someone or something?

- Optimism: Are you the kind of person that sees the glass half-full?
- Patience: When you're on a road trip, are you the one in the back seat asking "are we there yet?"
- Persuasiveness: Can you convince people to do something?
- Punctuality: Are you on time?
- Respect: Do you have the ability to deeply admire someone because of his or her abilities, qualities, or achievements?
- Thoroughness: When you clean your room, do you dust that one lampshade in the corner?
- Understanding: Are you sympathetically aware of other people's feelings and circumstances?

What qualities here best describe you?

Verbal Communication

We can all agree that being able to talk is a pretty important part of life. Your employer may ask you how good you are at doing it.

- Discuss a time when you had to assert yourself (speak up) in order to get a point across that was important to you.

ANALYSIS: You may communicate very well when everyone is in agreement, but if you cannot speak your mind when it means creating conflict, then your usefulness as a team member is limited. There is also a fine line between assertion and aggression, and you need to ensure the interviewer that you clearly know the difference.

- Have you had to "sell" an idea to your co-workers, classmates or group? How did you do it? Did they "buy" it?

ANALYSIS: In the world of work, the most common use of communication is to persuade someone to do something: buy something, sell something, complete something, or do something correctly. Are you good at it? Think of an example. If you absolutely can't think of one, and you're in the interview, and the clock is ticking, give a theoretical situation (I can't think of one off the top of my head, but if I did have to sell something, here's what I would say.)

- Give me an example of a time when you were able to successfully communicate with another person, even when that individual may not have personally liked you. How did you handle the situation? What obstacles or difficulties did you face? How did you deal with them?

ANALYSIS: The act of communication is about communicating with other people, and it is the most challenging when you are dealing with someone you don't like. What the interviewer is looking for in this answer is an acknowledgment that not all people are likable but that you can reign in your personal feelings for the sake of your job.

- How do you ensure that someone understands what you are saying?

ANALYSIS: The essence of this question is to learn if you recognize the importance of active listening and actually practicing the skill.

- Give me an example of a situation where proper communication allowed you to get the task/project done quickly.

- Tell me about a time when the ability to communicate effectively was critical to the success of a task or project. How did you handle it?
- Give me an example of a time when you had to explain a complicated procedure to someone who was new to the situation. What did you do? What were the results?
- Describe a recent situation when miscommunication created a problem.

ANALYSIS: Effective communication makes the workplace much more efficient, whether you're working as a host or a stock person. You should be able to give an example that demonstrates your understanding of this relationship. When communication fails, it can cause big problems at work.

If you're having a hard time thinking of a situation, try to think about school and school projects.

- Tell me about a time when you really had to pay attention to what someone else was saying, actively seeking to understand their message.
- Tell me about a time when your active listening skills were critical to the success of a project.
- Describe for me a situation where you missed some important details that were communicated to you. What was the outcome? How did you resolve the situation?

ANALYSIS: Many high-energy individuals have a bad habit of not listening carefully. If you have ever not listened carefully to a classmate, teacher, or supervisor before, let your interviewer know that you have since learned from the mistake.

Also, think about school. Was there ever a lecture that you had to listen to that was particularly difficult? A set of instructions that were very detailed and particular?

- Describe for me an instance when you jumped into a task or project before you fully understood the entire concept.

ANALYSIS: Poor listening is one of the easiest ways to create communication breakdown. Situation comedy writers rely on miscommunication for their source of humor. Fortunately, on TV, by the end of the 30 minutes, the situation gets resolved. In the workplace, it takes much longer and can cause a significant amount of damage to productivity and relationships. Ineffective listening happens all the time, so you want to demonstrate that you understand this fact and have learned how to avoid it.

- Tell me about a time when you worked with someone who was very difficult to understand. Perhaps the person's first language was not English or he had a disability that affected his ability to communicate. Explain how you overcame the situation.

ANALYSIS: Workplaces today are multicultural and inclusive of people with varying degrees of ability. The likelihood that an employee will need to communicate with a customer or co-worker who is hard to understand is very high. Use this question to detail the types of strategies you use in difficult situations. You might want to mention body language, other non-verbal clues, paraphrasing, summarizing, and asking questions.

- Your supervisor has given you instructions to complete a project. You are not clear as to some of the details of the instructions. What do you do?

ANALYSIS: Communicating with supervisors is slightly different than with co-workers. There is a level of responsibility and authority that needs to be respected, and the interviewer might use this question to determine how much you adjust your communication as it goes up the organization chart. The best way to answer this question is to focus on the importance of asking questions.

Interpersonal Skills

Interpersonal just means the relationship or communication between two people. When we talk about "interpersonal skills," we are talking about how good you are at communicating with another person.

- Describe the types of people you get along with best and why.
- How have you developed your interpersonal skills?
- Describe your relationship with the people you work with, whether at school, work, or a volunteering position.

ANALYSIS: These are good openers to get to know you, but they're a little tougher than the easy questions. Demonstrate that you understand that although a person may not like a co-worker, customer, or boss, he or she must develop coping mechanisms to ensure communication is clear and the work environment is pleasant.

- Describe the most difficult working relationship you've had with an individual. What specific actions did you take to improve the relationship? What was the outcome? (Your interviewer will not ask you this if you have no work experience.)
- Describe the types of people you have difficulty getting along with and why.
- Think about a difficult boss or teacher. What made him or her difficult? How did you successfully interact with this person?
- Describe how you handle rude, difficult, or impatient people.
- Describe a situation when you wished you had acted differently with someone at work or in class. What happened? What did you do about the situation?

ANALYSIS: The world of work is full of all sorts of people, and you need to demonstrate that you will be able to get along with and communicate effectively with everyone.

Be careful of how you discuss the scenario. You want to show that you know how to deal with challenging individuals. To do this, emphasize that you learned from your experiences and that you've come to appreciate differences. Don't talk about the traits that made that specific person or people difficult.

- Give me an example of a situation when you demonstrated sensitivity to diversity issues.
- Give me an example of your ability to communicate effectively and build relationships with people regardless of cultural differences.

ANALYSIS: Cultural differences are becoming more and more commonplace in the work environment. With all the other challenges to working well with other people, you certainly don't need ethnicity or cultural discrimination coming into play.

The desired answer to these questions is one that minimizes cultural differences and offers a tolerant view of the world and its people. Use politically correct terms for other cultures and races, and speak inclusively (as in, we are all in this together), rather than an "us" and "them" type of response.

The politically correct terms for other cultures and races are hard to pinpoint. However, there are phrases that are generally deemed appropriate.

Some examples of politically correct terms are: African American, Asian, gay, Hispanic, Latino/a, lesbian, and transgendered.

- One of your co-workers has a trait or habit that affects his relationships with other co-workers and customers. It is a difficult trait to mention, but you feel it must be brought to his or her attention. How do you handle the situation?

ANALYSIS: This question deals with your honesty and straightforwardness when dealing with other people. Make sure you can get your point across sensitively and considerately, while preserving the other person's dignity in the process. There are many self-proclaimed "tell-it-like-it-is" people who are upfront with others, but they come across as rude and insulting.

The effective communicator approaches the situation with empathy, putting himself or herself in the other person's shoes. The ineffective communicator just wants the other person to change regardless of that person's feelings or ability to change.

- It is often necessary to adjust our method or style of communicating to meet the needs of the individual or group we are addressing. Give me an example of a time when you used a different approach or interpersonal style to more effectively communicate with a peer.
- Describe a situation in which you were able to effectively "read" another person and guide your actions by your understanding of their needs and values.

ANALYSIS: The main part of interpersonal skills is the ability to change your responses to suit the situation and the person that you're dealing with. Demonstrate that you can use a different style to deal with different people.

- Some situations require us to express ideas or opinions in a very tactful and careful way. Tell me about a time when you were successful in this type of situation.

ANALYSIS: Tact refers to your sensitivity in dealing with others or with difficult issues. It is very important, and it is what constitutes the difference between honesty and rudeness. Consider talking about a time when you compromised.

Conflict Resolution Skills

We're all human. We don't agree on everything. We fight. The question is: how do you go about dealing with it? Are you respectful and mindful of the other person when dealing with arguments?

- In any field, conflicts will often arise between co-workers. How have you resolved a conflict with a co-worker or classmate?

- Describe a situation where you had a conflict with another individual and how you dealt with it. What was the outcome? How did you feel about it?
- Tell me about a situation where you were involved in a conflict. What did you do to resolve that conflict?
- Tell me about a difficult situation where it was desirable for you to keep a positive attitude.

ANALYSIS: Conflict is inevitable and relatively frequent. The actual conflict situation that you choose to relay is an excellent source of information about what really triggers your personal conflicts. Obviously, the resolution aspect of the question is important, but what you want to avoid is demonstrating that you view minor, everyday occurrences as conflicts requiring full-fledged conflict-resolution skills.

- Describe the way you handled a specific problem involving others with differing values, ideas, and beliefs in your previous job/in the classroom.
- Tell me about a time when you had to resolve a difference of opinion with a co-worker/classmate or supervisor/teacher. How do you feel you showed respect?

ANALYSIS: A difference of opinion or core values is very often the basis of conflict and the type that is most difficult to resolve. The way a person sets out to work with people who are fundamentally different than himself or herself says a great deal about the person's ability to deal with differences in general.

The bottom line is to maintain respect and professionalism at all times. These questions can yield valuable information about how you deal with core personality and value differences. If you can provide a solid example in this category, then chances are the interviewer will rate your conflict resolution skills at least above average.

- Tell me about a conflict you have had with a superior/teacher. How did you resolve the conflict? How did you work towards mending the relationship with that superior/teacher?
- Tell me about the manager/teacher/team leader who was the most difficult to work for. How did you handle this difficult relationship?

ANALYSIS: Conflicts with superiors should be kept to a minimum, and if and when they do occur, they must be handled with the utmost tact and respect. Demonstrate that you respect lines of authority, however informal, and operate within the system. If you have never had a conflict with a teacher, say so, but be sure to give a similar example, such as an argument with your parents (we've all had one of those, right?).

- Tell me about a time when you were assigned to a team that had a co-worker or classmate you did not particularly like. How did you manage to make the team project successful while dealing with your personal feelings?
- Give me an example of a situation where you had difficulties with a team member. What, if anything, did you do to resolve the difficulties?

ANALYSIS: Interpersonal skills are all the more important when working within a team environment, so it is important to demonstrate how you could effectively deal with conflict in this particular situation.

- Tell me about a time when you saw a potential conflict between yourself and another co-worker or classmate. What did you do to help prevent the conflict?

ANALYSIS: This question is designed to determine whether you believe "an ounce of prevention is worth a pound of cure." In other words, if you see something potentially bad about to happen, what do you do to stop it?

Empathy

Empathy looks a lot like the word "sympathy," which essentially means feeling bad for someone else. The difference is that empathy means that you can actually understand and share those feelings of misfortune with another person. Basically, empathy is sympathy on steroids.

The reason your future boss is asking you empathy-related questions is because he or she wants to know if you have a heart — well, at least in the business place.

- Give me an example of when you identified with someone else's difficulties at work or in class. What, if anything, did you do to help them?

ANALYSIS: With a question like this, an interviewer is looking for an answer that displays genuine concern for the other individual. People with natural empathy will focus on what the other person was going through, whereas people who are "faking it" will be less convincing and compelling.

Be careful when talking about an example that deals with a fellow employee's personal life; better answers are ones that highlight how you helped a co-worker or classmate with a job-related task or issue.

- Give me an example of when you went out of your way to help someone. What were your thoughts and feelings about that situation?

ANALYSIS: The candidate with a solid grasp of empathy will express thoughts and feelings such as self-satisfaction, accomplishment and enhanced self-esteem. People who generally embrace empathy do it for their own pleasure, rather than what they hope to gain from the situation. Emphasize how good you felt about the experience, and demonstrate that your actions were well received.

- Give me an example of when you had to make a decision where the choices were either in favor of your own self-interest or someone else's. What were your thoughts and feelings? What did you do?

ANALYSIS: There is no clear right or wrong answer, and it is confusing as well as stressful. Be honest. What will be important is a well-thought-out answer that talks about both choices and a solid argument for why one option was chosen over the other.

- What positive contributions have you made to your community or society?
- Give me an example of when you were given special recognition or acknowledgment for your contributions to the disadvantaged.

ANALYSIS: Depending on the culture or overall purpose of the organization you are interviewing at, this may be an important factor when considering employment. Every company places a different value on community service, community involvement, and other unselfish activities. This is one of the reasons that doing volunteer work is important — it not only benefits your community, but it can help you get a job. Consider working at your local soup kitchen or talking to the residents at a nearby nursing home one weekend.

- Can you recall a time when a person's cultural background affected your approach to a work situation?

ANALYSIS: Cultural differences are often at the root of many interpersonal conflicts at work. You must be able to demonstrate that you have a tolerance for differences in culture as well as opinion. Don't be afraid of this question, either. The best way to answer is to be honest about your initial thoughts, and then talk about how those changed as you got to know the person and their culture. Oftentimes, stereotypes unravel and you realize that people are not who you initially thought they might be.

Customer Service Situations

Even if you don't have any experience with customer service, you probably have a general idea of how it's done by being serviced your whole life. In other words, do you ever notice how your waitress or the cashier at the grocery store handles a problem? Draw on that experience to help you answer these questions.

- Describe the steps you would take if a customer came to you with a problem you could solve at your job level.

ANALYSIS: Customer complaints or concerns are perhaps the most difficult situations in which to display empathy, self-control, and a commitment to service. However, these are the exact traits that are required for any position that deals with the general public and customers. Actually solving the problem is not as important in this answer as the steps you took along the way.

The focus of a question like this should be on getting a manager. Oftentimes, the customer is interested in talking to someone with authority in the establishment. Your role is to smile, be polite, and be understanding. Smile and wave, folks. Smile and wave.

- Describe a situation where you were given exceptional customer service. What made it stand out?

ANALYSIS: In order to give excellent service, you need to recognize what outstanding service is. Think about a time when you went out to eat and you loved your server. Odds are it was their attitude — a smile can go a long way in the service industry. Your answer should demonstrate that you place value on helping a customer to feel satisfied, dignified, respected, understood and appreciated.

- Describe the steps you would take if a customer came to you with a problem that was beyond your knowledge and/or responsibilities.

ANALYSIS: Providing excellent customer service requires doing more than simply what you can do. Demonstrate that you recognize your own limitations in terms of authority, responsibility, or experience. No one expects you to know everything, so don't be afraid to ask someone to help you.

- Describe the steps you would use to calm an angry customer.

ANALYSIS: The general rule of thumb when it comes to dealing with an angry customer is to get the manager. That's part of the beauty of working an entry-level position in the service industry — when things go south fast, get the manager. In this question, you want to talk about how you would speak to the customer, which should be very reassuring. For example, "We will get this situation under control. Let me get my manager, and don't worry. We will take care of you."

- Why is follow-up important in customer service?
- A customer comes in with a small request. The small request is not a priority for you but you realize that they have the potential to use your services extensively in the future. How do you ensure that the customer has a good experience and will want to come back to you in the future?

ANALYSIS: The answer doesn't need to be an elaborate scheme where the customer is phoned or contacted a few days or weeks after the incident. It can simply be escorting the customer to the door, engaging in pleasant small talk, acknowledging the customer the next time he or she comes in, or anything else that actively promotes a positive end to the situation.

Problem Solving Skills

Being able to solve a problem is a huge part of having a job. Your employer may ask you how you have solved problems in the past or how you might solve them in this particular workplace.

- Describe a difficult problem that you tried to solve. How did you identify the problem? How did you go about trying to solve it?
- Think about a complex project or assignment that you have been assigned. What approach did you take to complete it?

ANALYSIS: Your answer should demonstrate that you apply a systematic problem-solving method. Show that you will not jump headfirst into the problem without taking the steps necessary to make sure that the actions are not going to contribute to the problem. Problem solving is stressful, and sometimes the immediate reaction is to go into "fix it" mode. Unfortunately, a problem cannot be fixed unless the causes and contributing factors have been identified.

Recognize that problem solving has two separate focuses: short-term and long-term. The short-term focus is on doing what needs to be done to get things up and running until the entire situation is dealt with. The long-term focus is on solving the problem and making sure it does not happen again.

- Describe for me a major project that you worked on where things did not go exactly as planned.
- Describe a time when you failed to solve a problem.

ANALYSIS: You may not like talking about your failures, but we all know that everyone has had them, and what is important is how you handled the situation. What did you learn from the experience? The focus here is not so much on what you did wrong, but how you internalized that information and used it, hopefully, to improve your performance in the future.

- Tell me about a problem that needed a fast response and how you handled it.

ANALYSIS: This question explores when and where you use good judgment in determining how quick of a response to a problem is needed. If a customer is in a rush and there is a problem, you need to be empathetic and think on your feet — your boss wants to know that you are capable of that.

- Tell me about a time when you missed an obvious solution to a problem.

ANALYSIS: Although this may be tough to admit, you want to be honest. Demonstrate that you learned from the situation and applied this knowledge in similar situations afterward.

- Tell me about a situation where when you were first presented with a problem, you had absolutely no idea how to approach it, and how you eventually solved the problem.
- Describe a situation in which you effectively developed a solution to a problem by combining different perspectives or approaches.
- Describe a recent situation in which you asked for advice or help.

ANALYSIS: Here, you should showcase your ability to be creative and innovative in problem solving. You also want to talk about how you have asked other people for help. Don't pretend like you can do everything on your own; none of us can.

Decision Making Skills

Has the following conversation ever happened to you?

> *Mom*: "Where do you want to go for dinner?"
>
> *You*: "I don't know."
>
> *Mom*: "Just pick a place."
>
> *You*: "I don't care."
>
> *Mom:* "Any place."
>
> *You:* "I don't know."
>
> *Mom:* "Anywhere you want."
>
> *You:* "What is there?"
>
> *Mom:* "What do you mean, what is there?"
>
> *You:* "Give me some choices."
>
> *Mom:* "You know what there is."
>
> *You:* "Well, I don't know."

If so, don't bring it up in the interview — your boss wants to know that you are capable of making decisions, and the right ones, at that.

- What was the biggest decision you made in the past three months? Tell me about the process you went through to make it.
- Give me an example of a time you had to make a difficult decision.
- What is the most difficult decision you've had to make? How did you arrive at your decision? What was the result?

ANALYSIS: The purpose of these types of questions is to get you talking about how you go about making decisions. What type of analysis do you use? Where does prior learning and experience fit in? Do you have a track record of success? Ultimately, you want to show that you make solid, well-thought-out decisions when faced with difficult circumstances.

- Recall for me a time when you had to choose between several alternatives. How did you evaluate each alternative?
- When you evaluate different choices, what are the criteria you use? Give me a specific example.
- Tell me about the tools and techniques you use to help your decision-making process.

ANALYSIS: A difficult decision is one where there are valid alternatives from which to choose. What separates a good decision maker from an average, or even poor one, is the ability to choose the best option. Demonstrate the analytical and problem-solving processes you employ.

- Tell me about the riskiest decision that you have made.

ANALYSIS: Risk exponentially increases the difficulty of making a decision. Risk also tends to delay decision-making. A good answer will show balance between analyzing the problem and taking action.

- Describe a recent unpopular decision you made. How was it received? How did you handle it?

ANALYSIS: It is extremely difficult to make an unpopular decision or one that is doubted. The only way the decision is successfully defended is if the analysis has been done and the alternatives clearly evaluated. Show that you did dot all the i's and cross all the t's.

Another important element of this question is interpersonal skills. It is difficult to keep composure when you feel attacked or questioned.

Discuss your method for dealing with the criticism and make sure it was appropriate.

- Give me an example of a time when you had to be quick in coming to a decision.
- What kind of decisions do you make rapidly? What kind takes more time? Give examples.
- Describe a situation where you handled decisions under pressure.

ANALYSIS: Time pressures provide a prime influence for making fair or even poor decisions. Quick decision-making is one thing; preparing for and handling the consequences is quite another. Make sure that you demonstrate that you use the time available to you to evaluate your options when making a quick decision.

- Describe a time in which you weighed the pros and cons of a situation and decided not to take action, even though you were under pressure to do so.
- Tell me about a time when you took a public stance on an issue and then had to change your position.

ANALYSIS: This is another question that judges your commitment levels to your decision-making processes. Those who use a well-planned, thorough, and well-executed process have no reason to second-guess themselves.

- Tell me about a time when you had to make a decision without all the information you needed. How did you handle it? Why? Were you happy with the outcome?

- Give me an example of a time when you had to keep from speaking or making a decision because you did not have enough information.

ANALYSIS: While there is always a level of uncertainty in decision-making, sometimes a person is forced to make a decision even when there is a glaring hole in the analysis. These types of questions will be evaluating your overall experience with decision-making. The process will not be thorough, so you need to demonstrate how well you can depend on judgment and past experience to make reasonable decisions.

- Tell me about a decision you made in the past that later proved to be a wrong decision. Why was it wrong? What would you do differently now, if anything, in making that decision?
- Tell me about a situation where you made a poor decision and had to live with the consequences.

ANALYSIS: Accepting responsibility for a poor decision is hard, and no one wants to admit in an interview that he or she actually made a poor decision. However, what you need to focus on is how you dealt with the consequences. Do not give excuses or spread the blame. Show that you can stand behind good decisions as well as bad ones. Be sure to discuss what you learned from the situation.

Teamwork Skills

Particularly in a restaurant, teamwork is everything. If the staff isn't working together, things won't go smoothly. Your employer wants to know how well you do when it comes to working with other people.

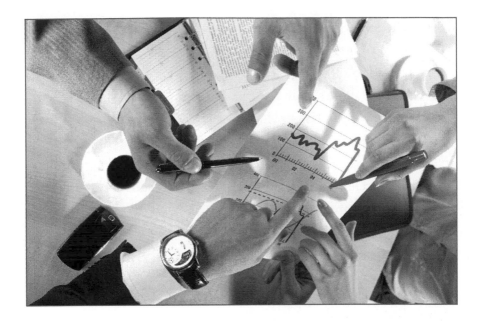

- Describe a time when you were a member of a team or group that had to achieve a goal or solve a problem. What type of team or group was it? What was the team or group trying to do? What was your role? How did you contribute to the team or group? Was the team or group successful?
- Can you give me an example of a team decision you were involved in recently? What did you do to help the team reach the decision?
- What have you done in past situations to contribute toward a team environment?
- Describe a project you were responsible for that required a lot of interaction with people over a long period of time.
- Tell me about a time when you had to rely on a team to get things done.
- Describe a group project you have had to do.

- Describe the types of teams you've been involved with. What were your roles?
- Describe a team experience you found rewarding.
- Tell me about a course, work experience or extracurricular activity where you had to work closely with others. How did it go? How did you overcome any difficulties?
- Think of a time when you worked effectively in a team situation. Describe how you felt about the contributions of the others on the team.
- Tell me about a time when, if it hadn't been for teamwork, your goal might not have been achieved.

ANALYSIS: All of these questions are designed to get you talking about what being a member of a team means to you. Notions of teamwork are very diverse, and you need to showcase your point of view on the subject. Discuss what you think teamwork is, your idea of cooperation, what role you assume in a team situation (are you the leader or the follower?), what qualifies as an effective team, and what makes a team experience enjoyable.

Most people realize that teamwork is expected, but not all people appreciate the difficulties that are involved with teamwork. Sometimes, it's easier to accomplish a task on your own, but the result will not be as good as the one that an effective team accomplishes. Show that you appreciate teamwork for what it can add to a work environment.

- Tell me about one of the toughest teams/groups you've had to work with. What made it difficult? What did you do?

- Sometimes it can be frustrating when trying to get information from other people so that you can solve a problem. Please describe a situation you've had like this. What did you do?
- Tell me about a time when you worked with a classmate or co-worker who was not doing their share of the work. How did you handle it?
- Describe a team experience you found disappointing. What would you have done to improve the outcome?

ANALYSIS: Working closely with other people who have different values, styles, expertise, experience, perceptions, and work ethics is very difficult. Talk about how great you are at being empathetic (remember that word?). Effective team members present conflict as a shared dynamic and focus more on the solutions than the problems.

- Give me an example of when you were on a team that failed to meet its objectives. What could the team have done differently?

ANALYSIS: This question is designed to get you to think objectively about the team's overall performance. Take adequate responsibility for the failure and discuss your performance and how it contributed to the ineffectiveness. Be sure to mention what you learned from the situation and how you will apply that knowledge in the future.

Also, this doesn't mean that entire project had to be a failure. Maybe it's easier to think of one aspect of the project that could have been better (maybe the presentation was too short or the introduction was boring). Talk about what you could have done to improve that one thing.

- Gaining the cooperation of others can be difficult. Give a specific example of when you had to do that and what challenges you faced. What was the outcome? What was the long-term impact on your ability to work with this person?

- Describe how you felt about a decision the team wanted to make that you didn't agree with.
- Describe a situation where the team was having trouble agreeing on a decision and what you did to help.
- Describe a situation in which you had to arrive at a compromise or help others to compromise. What was your role? What steps did you take? What was the result?

ANALYSIS: One of the main challenges of working within a team is compromising. Everyone has different ideas, and part of being a team is being able to take bits and pieces of everyone's ideas and putting them all together.

The whole idea of teamwork is to bring together different opinions and perspectives in the hopes of creating a better outcome than any one person could come up with. These interpersonal differences are what make coming to an agreement so difficult. Showcase your appreciation of these differences, and discuss the strategies you use to handle them.

- Tell me about a time where you were a member of a team and had to encourage everyone to participate.
- Give me an example of something you did that helped build enthusiasm in others.

ANALYSIS: If you're a cheerleader, these questions are your time to shine. The interviewer is trying to determine how much spirit and enthusiasm you bring to a team situation. Some people are very comfortable in a motivational or inspirational role and others are not. If you aren't, that's

OK. Your employer doesn't expect you to have every great customer service attribute known to man. Make up for this in other areas of the interview, but don't tell your boss that you're enthusiastic if you aren't. That's a little difficult to fake, especially if you plan on working there for a while.

Organization Skills

Are you the one with the labeled folders and the color-coordinated flashcards? Or are you the one that jams all your papers in the bottom of your backpack, and when your teacher asks you to get out that worksheet from last week, you realize you have no idea where it is? If you're the first one, your employer will love you. If you're the second one, you have a little bit of work to do.

- Are you able to schedule your time? How far ahead can you schedule?
- Can you walk me through last week and tell me how you planned the week's activities and how the schedule worked out?
- Describe a time in school when you had many projects or assignments due at the same time. What steps did you take to get them all done?
- What have you done in order to be effective with your organization and planning?
- Give me an example of when your ability to manage your time and priorities proved to be an asset.
- Tell me about a project that you planned. How did you organize and schedule the tasks? Tell me about your action plan.

ANALYSIS: With these questions, the interviewer is trying to learn more about your use of organizational tools. Demonstrate that you are flexible enough to adapt to the situation at hand.

Discuss the amount of time you spend planning. Neglecting the planning phase is detrimental to productivity, but so is over-planning. People who plan every detail may have trouble adapting to change and may spend more time organizing their work than actually doing their work.

- Describe a time when you had to handle multiple responsibilities and how you managed it.
- How do you prioritize projects and tasks when scheduling your time? Give me some examples.

ANALYSIS: Choosing what needs to get done first can be difficult. In any job, there are going to be times when there is more than one thing that needs to be done. For example, if you are a server and one table needs their check, another table needs refills, and another one needs their food, you need to be able to prioritize. Which one is the most important right now? The best way to talk about this is to explain what you did or what you would do first and why. As long as you have a reason for your answer, you're good to go.

- Has your time schedule ever been upset by unforeseen circumstances? Give me a recent example. What did you do then?

ANALYSIS: The best plans are inevitably put to the test. Let the interviewer know that you anticipate this type of change and build in contingency plans or extra time to accommodate possible change. Your example can be really simple. For example: "I had a paper due on Tuesday, but I had to miss school because I was sick. Since I couldn't turn it in in person, I emailed the file to my school." Something as simple as this will get the job done.

- Tell me about a time when you were given a deadline by someone of higher authority which could not possibly be met. How did you handle it?
- Tell me about the last project you worked on that had a fixed deadline.

- Describe for me a time when you missed a deadline. What was the result and what did you learn from the experience?
- Can you tell me about a time when you rushed the completion of a project, sacrificing the quality of the final product?

ANALYSIS: Deadlines are inevitable and can be stress inducing if you don't plan right. Show that you know how to handle deadlines, and talk about what factors contributed to missed deadlines. Also be sure to talk about how important quality is. Quality over quantity, as the saying goes.

Motivation

Being motivated in life is really important; it's how we reach our goals. Your employer wants to know that you're motivated, especially when it comes to doing the job.

- Tell me about an important goal that you set in the past. Were you successful? Why?
- Give me an example of when you have worked the hardest and felt the greatest sense of achievement.
- Give me an example of when you took a risk to achieve a goal. What was the outcome?
- What were your objectives for last year? Were they achieved? How?

ANALYSIS: When you answer these questions, try to show how likely you are to actually set goals for yourself. Some people are very good at achieving goals that are set for them, but those people who actively set their own goals are the ones who are continuously striving to improve and perform at higher levels than expected. Also talk about how you track your progress.

- Describe a situation when you were able to have a positive influence on the actions of others.
- Relate a scenario where you were responsible for motivating others.

ANALYSIS: Motivating yourself is one thing, motivating others is quite another. What you want to demonstrate is that you are able to remain upbeat and enthusiastic about goals.

- What are your standards of success in your job/school? What have you done to meet these standards?

ANALYSIS: If your grades aren't the best, talk about how hard you work. Give examples of how much time you put into your school work or how attentive you are in class.

- Give an example of when your persistence had the biggest payoff. Give me an example of when you achieved something by your persistence that others couldn't.
- Please describe a time when you were successful at an activity only after repeated attempts.
- Describe a situation in which you persevered with an idea or a plan even when others disagreed with you.

ANALYSIS: Persistence means that you keep trying to do something no matter how hard it gets. Having this quality is the sign of a really motivated person, but there is such a thing is going too far. There are people who persevere even when the end result is so longer valid or relevant.

These people, though highly motivated, are misguided and may not be the most productive people. You should demonstrate that you are persistent when it comes to meeting work goals.

- Give examples of your experiences at school or in a job that were satisfying.
- Give me an example of a time when a project really excited you.
- Under what conditions do you work best?

ANALYSIS: These questions are designed to uncover what external factors you consider motivating. Self-motivation is wonderful, but we all need to work in an environment that is pleasing and enjoyable. Figure out what it is about a situation that makes it satisfying for you, and then answer the question.

- Tell me about a time when you were given an assignment that was distasteful or unpleasant.
- Tell me what your least favorite part or parts are of your most recent assignment.

ANALYSIS: It is easy to get motivated by a project or situation that is interesting and exciting, but the true test of your motivation is how you react when the circumstances are less than inviting. Every job carries a certain number of elements that are boring, and you need to show that you can find something motivating about the situation even if it is just the thought of finishing.

- Describe a really tough or long day and how you dealt with it.
- How have you motivated yourself to complete an assignment or task that you did not want to do?
- Describe a time when you were unmotivated to get a job done.

- Have you found any ways to make school or a job easier or more rewarding?

ANALYSIS: These questions are designed to uncover your ability to self-motivate. Tell the interviewer what you value and feel is important for your own satisfaction.

- Describe a situation where you were asked to assume responsibility for something you had never handled before.

ANALYSIS: Here is a question that involves motivation and confidence. An ideal answer is one that includes some nervousness but overall excitement and honor at being given the responsibility. High motivation levels are excellent, but they have to be kept in check by a realistic sense of what you are and are not capable of doing with the skills and resources available. Your answer should include seeking outside assistance and expertise to complete the task as well as the typical strategies of goal setting and intrinsic rewards. There is a fine line between being motivated and "up" for anything and biting off more than you can chew.

Initiative

How willing are you to take charge before other people do? Are you ready to take things into your own hands? If you have initiative, your employer wants to know.

- Give an example of a time when you went above and beyond the call of duty.
- Describe a time when you decided on your own that something needed to be done, and you took on the task to get it done.

- How have you demonstrated initiative? Tell me about a time when you demonstrated the most initiative.
- Tell me about a project you initiated. What did you do? Why? What was the outcome? Were you happy with the result?

ANALYSIS: These classic initiative prompts will provide valuable information about what specific activities you feel are "above and beyond the call of duty." Make sure it's actually something significant, or your future employer may question how much initiative you really have.

- Tell me about a time when your initiative caused a change to occur.
- Give me an example of a situation that could not have happened successfully without you being there.
- What was the best idea you came up with during your school career? How did you apply it?

ANALYSIS: This is your opportunity to show how useful your suggestions for improvement really are. Your job is to talk about good your ideas are; you want to impress your interview.

Stress Management

Managing stress can be really tough. After all, interviewing itself is stressful. Your boss wants to know how you handle stress, and she may evaluate this as part of the overall interview process, but she also may come right out and ask you about it with questions like these.

- Describe a project or goal that has caused you frustration.
- Describe situations that you have been under pressure in which you feel you handled well.
- What do you do to manage stress?
- Describe how you work when you are under pressure.

ANALYSIS: All of these questions are designed to help the interviewer understand your how you deal with stress. Make sure you're giving details. Saying something broad like "I take stress day by day" is not going to give your interview an idea of how well you handle stress.

Give really specific examples, such as "When I have a stressful day ahead, I make a checklist. As I go through the day, I check off everything I have completed, which eases my stress." This kind of specific response can be applied to any task. Avoid talking about anything you consume to ease stress (you know, that gallon of chocolate ice cream).

- What are your stress triggers?
- How do you know when you are under stress?

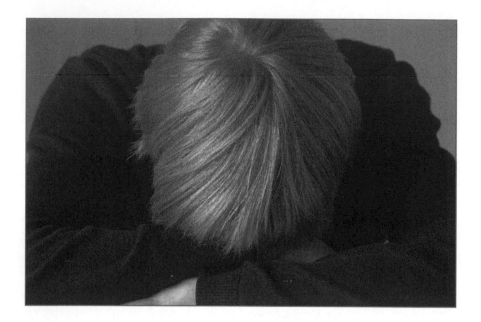

ANALYSIS: Often the first and most important component of dealing with stress is recognizing what causes it for you. For example, if you get stressed out by too many tasks, you can say "being overwhelmed stresses me out." Don't be afraid to answer this question; odds are, your stress triggers are shared by your interviewer.

- Who do you go to for support when you are stressed or under pressure at work or school?
- After a difficult day, how do you alleviate your stress?
- Tell me about a time when you were under stress and a co-worker or classmate stepped in to help you.

ANALYSIS: Having outlets for stress relief is very important, and you need to show that you are able to ask for and use the assistance available to you. Co-workers and family members are common sources of stress relief, but exercise clubs or other hobby groups are often useful as well.

Show how varied your approach to stress management is. The more resources you employ, the higher the likelihood of success.

- How would you handle the pressure of dealing with a very angry customer, co-worker or other person you encounter on the job?
- Describe a time when you lost your temper.
- Describe a situation when you had to exercise a significant amount of self-control.

ANALYSIS: It's hard to be professional when there's an angry customer in your face. However, talk about staying calm and if you've lost your temper before, talk about what you learned from the situation.

Big Picture or Broad Questions

It's likely that your interviewer will ask questions like the ones above that are really specific. However, it's also possible that they'll ask you a really broad question that can seem harder to answer. An example of a question like this is: "Tell me about yourself."

Where do you even begin? With this one, you want to make sure that your answer reflects the fact that you're in a job interview, not on a blind date.

Talk about what school you go to, what grade you're in, what hobbies and interests you have, what sports you play, and what qualities you have that you think would make you a great candidate for the job. For example, an answer might go like this.

"My name is Anna, I'm a junior, and I go to the public school. I love singing and I play basketball. I'm really detail-oriented and have always been told that I'm good at reading people."

Keep in mind that this response is short and to the point. Anna hits on all of the main points without dragging on about anything. This lets the interview work with her answer by asking her to talk about something more if he or she is interested. For example, "Oh really? What kind of singing do you do?"

CHAPTER FIVE

How to Answer Tough Questions

While most of the questions listed in the previous chapter have an analysis with them that help you answer them, there are some general tips that will help you with the overall answering process.

Think

Even if you've studied all of the questions and have all your answers prepared and ready to go, odds are, you'll forget at least one when the time comes. Don't spout off the first thing that comes to mind when you get stuck. Sit back, relax, and give yourself a few seconds to compose yourself.

Your boss isn't going to think you're unprepared when you do this. In fact, many professional interviews have this thinking time as part of the interview process. For example, when you interview to be a police officer, you are given three minutes to answer each question. You are allowed to use all three minutes to think and answer — the thinking process is built into the time allowance.

Be Concise

Not every answer needs to be a paragraph long. Answer the question in as little words as you can. If you go into a question thinking you need to elaborate, you may get stuck and start to feel overwhelmed.

If you have the urge to tell a story related to a question, don't. Your interviewer just wants to get to know you, not your whole life story.

There is beauty in simplicity, and your interviewer will appreciate how eloquent you can be with your words. (Eloquent means that you're really good at talking.)

Don't Say "Um"

Almost all of us have had an encounter with the famous "um." And it isn't just a useless word; according to Herbert Clark of Stanford University, words and phrases like "uh," "um," and "you know" have meaning in our speech. It's a way of letting the other person know that we're thinking: "If we anticipate a delay in our speech, we choose the appropriate sound to signal this to the listener. These phrases mean 'I need to make sure you realize I'm delaying because I'm having trouble.'"

However, these words can make a bad impression and can make you seem unprepared. Two ways to minimize how much you may end up using these words are: prepare your answers beforehand, and use a few seconds to think about your answer before speaking.

Be Yourself

When it comes to answering the questions, always be true to yourself. Don't say you're organized if you aren't, but bring a positive side to the statement by saying that you're working on it or that you've been taking specific steps to becoming better.

If a question is asked about a specific situation, and you can't think of one, explain how you would act if it did happen. For example: "Well,

I've never had to deal with a rude co-worker, but if I did in the future, this is what I would do."

Everything you say should be based on reality. Your interviewer wants to get to know you, and if you make up situations that aren't based on anything in real life, they'll eventually find out.

Speak With Confidence

You have prepared your answers, and you're confident; show it through the way you speak. Speak loud enough so that the other person can hear you (nothing makes you seem more wimpy than a small, quiet voice), look directly in the interviewers eyes, and smile.

By using your voice, your eye contact, and your smile, you'll be beaming with confidence and your interviewer will be impressed. Even if one of your answers comes out a little lame, the fact that you're confident will help mask it.

Try Practicing/Roleplaying

You're familiar with the questions you'll be asked, you've thought about your answers, and you have so much interview advice flowing through you that it's spilling out your ears. Still don't feel like you're ready? It's all right. Read the sample interview below and you'll feel so prepared, you won't know what to do with yourself.

Sample Interview

APPLICANT: Charlie Davis
POSITION: Cashier

INTERVIEWER: "Hello Charlie, I'm Dianna. We spoke on the phone. I'm pleased to meet you in person. Were my directions OK?"

INTERVIEWEE: "Oh yes, I found the place with no problem."

INTERVIEWER: "Great. We're ready to get started so just follow me."

INTERVIEWEE: "Sure."

INTERVIEWER: "I know we discussed the fact that two of us will be doing the interview. Don't worry, we're not here to intimidate you; we simply find it's very valuable to get more than one opinion on a person's suitability."

INTERVIEWEE: "I understand, and I've been preparing for the interview."

INTERVIEWER: "Charlie, I'd like you to meet Greg. Greg is the direct supervisor of the position for which you are applying. He and I will be conducting the interview together. Are you ready to get started?"

INTERVIEWEE: "Sure, as ready as I'll ever be."

INTERVIEWER: "Oh, one last thing: In order for us to remember your responses we will be taking notes. Please don't let that distract you."

INTERVIEWEE: "OK."

INTERVIEWER: "OK, let's start by having you telling us a bit more about yourself. Tell me something that I wouldn't know just from reviewing your résumé."

INTERVIEWEE: "Well, I have two younger sisters. As the big brother, I like to get involved with the activities they like, so I have been learning a lot about ballet."

INTERVIEWER: "Thanks for sharing that with us. Can you tell me why you are applying for this job?"

INTERVIEWEE: "Sure, I've been looking to start working part time and get experience in customer service.

INTERVIEWER: "So what is the most important element you require in a job?"

INTERVIEWEE: "Although I have volunteered extensively in the past few years, I really want to learn more about the workplace, so I want a job where I know I will be learning."

INTERVIEWER: "How do you know when you've done a good job?"

INTERVIEWEE: "I know when I do a good job because I feel like I did everything I could in the situation. I don't need someone else to be constantly telling me what a good job I did, although that's nice every so often. I can tell in myself when I've worked hard at a job and done my best."

INTERVIEWER: "Tell me about a time when you knew you did an exceptional job and no one commented specifically on it."

INTERVIEWEE: "Actually, it was just last week. The organization I volunteer for was having a big fundraising event and we were short staffed. Even though my shift setting up was over, I decided to stay throughout the event to ensure everything ran smoothly. No one ever acknowledged that, but I was still glad that I stayed to help out."

The interview is underway and now the interviewer may start asking competency-focused questions. These questions are behavioral-based and require specific examples for each answer. Try to build a comfortable interview environment and give honest, straightforward answers.

INTERVIEWER: "That's great. In the role of cashier, you will be required to communicate with customers regularly. How would you rate your communication skills?"

INTERVIEWEE: "I would give myself an eight. I haven't had experience working with customers in this exact setting before, but I have frequently communicated with the attendees of events my volunteer organization has put on. Because they are our donors, we have been trained to communicate effectively with them and quickly deal with any concerns they have."

INTERVIEWER: "Tell me about how you communicate with your current supervisor concerning project processes, concerns, and suggestions."

INTERVIEWEE: "Well, I try to keep my supervisor very well informed. I work as her assistant so she needs to know where I am at as we plan different events. We have an arrangement where I can come to her with any questions and concerns and she requires a weekly update on my progress."

INTERVIEWER: "What about suggestions you may have? How do you communicate those ideas?"

INTERVIEWEE: "I try not to spring things on her. I think my ideas through, and then if they truly make sense, I ask for a meeting. That way I have time to prepare my suggestion, and I know she has time to hear what I am saying."

INTERVIEWER: "Communication is often a key stumbling block for a project's success. Give me an example of a situation where proper communication allowed you to get a project done quickly."

INTERVIEWEE: "That happened a few months ago. The faculty supervisor of the club I am president of asked me to make up a letter to give to all the homeroom teachers of the members of our club. I knew that would be a pretty time-consuming undertaking, because there are a lot of members in our organization. I asked her the purpose of the letter, and she said it was to alert members that elections would be the following week. When she said it, I realized that we could just announce the information on the school's morning announcement. By asking that one question, I saved a lot of time and was able to get the information out in a much more efficient manner."

Charlie did not appear to need many explanations, and his answers to the communication questions were quite good. Certainly no red flags were raised, and the interviewer probed for more specific information regarding how the applicant actually used good communication to work efficiently.

INTERVIEWER: "There are many employees in our organization and you will work with many of them. Please tell me about the relationships you have with key people at your current workplace."

INTERVIEWEE: "Well, I don't have a workplace exactly right now, but I do work with a couple of other volunteers at the nonprofit I help out at. I work mainly with my supervisor and two other volunteers, one of which I go to school with. My boss and I have a good relationship — she really understands how passionate I am about our organization, and she is always receptive to my fundraising ideas. She is also a generally positive person, so she doesn't bring the mood down if she is having difficultly with something. My relationship with the volunteer that is also my classmate is pretty good. We both really love working at the organization and actually have a lot of classes together in school. We try to help each other out, and it's a very give-and-take relationship. The other volunteer, on the other hand, is a little more difficult to get along with. He tends to be moody and quite focused on his own specific duties. Not so much a team player, which I prefer to work with. I think our main difference is that, while I volunteer because I like to, he volunteers to get service hours for school. Having said that, though, we do have a respectful relationship; it is just much more business-like and curt than other relationships I have at the organization."

INTERVIEWER: "Tell me more about this relationship you have with the second volunteer. Can you describe the last time you encountered difficulty? What happened and what was the result?"

INTERVIEWEE: "It was last week actually. It was at that same big event that I mentioned earlier. He was also only signed up to help set up the event. When some of our volunteers fell through, it was clear to me that we would have to step in to help run the rest of the event. I asked him if he would be able to stay and work with me. He snapped, "I finished what I said I would." I explained the situation to him, but he said he had other things to do with his time. I, too, had a couple of assignments for class that I could have worked on, but I felt that helping out was the right thing to do. However, I let it go and just asked a couple of friends that I knew could use the service hours if they would like to come out and help."

INTERVIEWER: "Can you tell me about another time you had difficulties with someone other than him? What was the situation and how did you handle it?"

INTERVIEWEE: "Well, recently I was working with a man from another company to see about renting a tent for our upcoming 5k race. At first, negotiations on the price of the tent were going fine, but then he found out that I was just a student volunteer and tried to hike the price way over our budget. I tried to get him to compromise, but he refused. I guess he thought that because I was just a student, I wouldn't know a reasonable price from an unreasonable one. The situation just wasn't working out, so I let my supervisor know and she took care of the tent rental instead. In the future, I believe we will be using a different company."

This portion of the interview yielded some very interesting facts about Charlie and the way he deals with people. It seems he gets along very well with people when there are no issues to deal with or when the person is a good match for his personality. He also demonstrated that he is relatively good at handling conflict and knows when to hand the situation off to a superior.

INTERVIEWER: "In this role, you will be working with a variety of people. Can you tell me about a time when you needed to understand another person's cultural background in order to work effectively with him or her?"

INTERVIEWEE: "Actually, at school we just got a transfer student from Australia. She is in my English class and we were assigned to the same group for a project. At first, her work ethic really bothered me. She was too relaxed and too methodical for me, and I found myself getting irritated. She was doing her part of the project fine, she just wasn't doing them with the same zest that I would have, and I knew it was my issue, not hers. Since I'd never been to Australia or knew any Australians, I invited her join my friends during our lunch period, and we got to talking about her culture and what life was like "down under." Turns out she was equally perplexed by our American vigor — things in Australia move at a slower pace and there is not that sense of urgency we experience here. I felt so good after talking with her, and now I understand where she is coming from."

INTERVIEWER: "As a cashier, you will often be asked for help by our customers. I'm interested in understanding your approach when dealing with people who may not be satisfied with your responsiveness."

INTERVIEWEE: "Hmmm, I must say that I am very responsive to people's requests. I think it is important to keep everyone satisfied."

INTERVIEWER: "OK, but what I'm really interested in hearing is a specific incident where someone made a request of you that maybe you didn't have time for or couldn't get to. How did the negative feedback make you feel and what did you do?"

INTERVIEWEE: "There was this one time when one of our donors called up the organization I volunteer for to complain about the seat she was assigned for our upcoming dinner event. She did not like one of the couples that would be at her table and wanted to be switched. However, the tables were organized by the amount donated, with people who donated more being seated at a table closer to the stage. I definitely did not have the authority to move her to a different table, and couldn't transfer her to a superior because they were all busy. I asked if I might be able to call her back later with a resolution, but she was not particularly happy with that suggestion. Although I did not want to, I ended up interrupting one of my superiors to have her handle the situation. Things ended up working out for the best, but the situation did make me feel very uncomfortable."

Notice how Charlie tried to avoid the "negatively" slanted customer service question. While you may tempted to do this, it is always better to give an honest answer. His example about the donor demonstrated once again that he understands when a conflict has gotten out of hand and has to be handed over to a superior to be dealt with. The one negative about his answer would be his slight negative description of the donor. Instead of saying she called to complain, it might sound better to the interviewer if he said that she called to discuss an issue. You do not want to make it seem that you tend to lay blame on the customer.

INTERVIEWER: "Charlie, can you tell me about a time when you had to make a decision very fast? What was the situation and outcome?"

INTERVIEWEE: "Oh gosh, fast decisions scare me, but I know sometimes you have no choice. Well, certainly the decision to stay and help out at that event we were understaffed for was quick, but it was helpful to the organization and I was able to finish my schoolwork the following day."

In this situation, the interviewer recognizes quickly that Charlie doesn't have much experience with quick decision-making. However, in the case of the position he is interviewing for, this is often not a problem. In the position of cashier, Charlie will be trained to deal with the most common problems that cashiers of this particular store typically have, and any other problems that come up will probably need to be addressed by his manager. However, this is not always the case. Other jobs you may choose to apply for may require good decision making skills, so consider whether or not that is something you are comfortable doing.

INTERVIEWER: "We send out our shift schedule the Saturday before the next work week. Tell me how you would plan out your week to make sure you could cover all your shifts."

INTERVIEWEE: "Well, thankfully, my volunteering schedule is very flexible, so I would work that schedule around this one. I use my calendar on my smartphone to keep track of all of my appointments and volunteering shifts, so I would continue to use that system for keeping track of my work schedule."

INTERVIEWER: "What exact types of activities do you track in your smartphone calendar?"

INTERVIEWEE: "I use it to write deadlines for school projects, meetings for clubs, and fundraising events for my volunteer organization. I like to have those reminders so I don't forget to do something important or miss a deadline or meeting or something."

INTERVIEWER: "Well, that brings me to my next question. Can you describe for me a time when you did miss a deadline? What happened and what was the result?"

INTERVIEWEE: "Well, it doesn't happen very often, but a few months ago I had several projects to work on all at once, and I was a day late submitting an assignment for my history class. I had the deadline in my calendar, but I got so busy with my other work that I just completely forgot about it. Thankfully, I was able to talk to my teacher about my situation and she gave me an extension. It was my first time turning something in late, so she was very forgiving. What I've done since then is set reminders for each of my deadlines and important other dates.

Now, the day before a deadline or event I have noted in my calendar, I get a message on my smartphone reminding me of it."

INTERVIEWER: "Besides your smartphone calendar, do you use any other planning tools on a regular basis?"

INTERVIEWEE: "No, not really. My smartphone is really all I need. It works for me and now that I can't miss seeing my deadlines, I haven't had a problem. I am a naturally very organized person — you should see my room — so my smartphone is my way of backing up the information that I store in my brain."

INTERVIEWER: "Can you relate for me a time when you had to cut corners in order to complete a project on time?"

INTERVIEWEE: "I'm not the type who cuts corners. There are times when I realize I didn't get everything done in a day that needed to be done so I just stay late and complete the work properly. I am very committed to my grades and my volunteer work and I will put in whatever time is necessary to complete the job properly. I have a strong work ethic, and I don't see myself ever being able to sacrifice quality for speed."

In this section of questions, Charlie is able to turn a negative answer (missing a project deadline) into a positive about what he learned. His use of reminders seems to work well for him, and the fact that the situation he describes is the only time he has missed a deadline is certainly a point in his favor.

While it is good that Charlie uses some sort of system to organize his life, the fact that he only uses one organizational system might be a negative in the eyes of the interviewer. He plans for deadlines and major events, but he makes no mention of daily task planning or prioritization. It is interesting to note that the last question in the section affirms why effective planning is so important. If Charlie did use a daily to-do list or some other prioritization process, he would not have to stay up late to complete his work.

INTERVIEWER: "Charlie, I'd like to switch gears a bit and get to know a little more about you and specifically what you find motivating."

INTERVIEWEE: "I love responsibility. I am really motivated when I know my volunteering supervisor trusts me to complete my work and doesn't feel the need to check up on me or hover over me. Not that I don't take direction well, because I do. I just work my best when it's on me to ask questions and for clarification rather than my supervisor assuming I need help or assistance when I don't. I think I'm also like a lot of other people in that I like to hear that I'm doing a good job or that my work is appreciated. No one needs to take out a big ad in the paper but a genuine 'thank you' every once in a while certainly makes me want to work extra hard."

INTERVIEWER: "So, tell me about the last time you felt really unmotivated to do something."

INTERVIEWEE: "Well, I guess every month when I know I have to create the meeting agenda for the club I'm president of, I cringe inside. Although I love the club, it's not my favorite task. But I know it has to be done, so I set up a little competition with myself. I came up with the idea when I realized I was getting the agenda done later and later. I set a time that I have to have it all written up — there are no excuses and no second chances — and if I get it done in time, I treat myself to a milkshake from my favorite ice cream shop. I've been doing it for a couple months now and it has helped immensely."

INTERVIEWER: "Describe for me the things you have liked about your volunteer organization and clubs."

INTERVIEWEE: "As I said before, responsibility is really important. I've also been fortunate enough to have been able to work with a team of people in both my volunteering position and in my school club that, for the most part, are just as dedicated to doing a good job as I am. I hate when I'm working in a group, like for a group project in school, where my team members just don't care and I have to end up doing the majority of the work."

INTERVIEWER: "Our office is based on the team approach, so I would like to hear about a situation where you motivated others to complete an assignment or to do a good job."

INTERVIEWEE: "I think I motivate others just with my optimism and positive outlook. I really try not to bring negativity when I'm working with a team. I like to demonstrate what I think is the right attitude to have toward assigned responsibilities."

INTERVIEWER: "Can you describe a specific situation where you did something overt, or beyond just displaying a positive attitude, to motivate someone else?"

INTERVIEWEE: "I guess what I do is use a lot of praise and encouragement and try to pay extra attention to the person in order to cheer them up. Like last week I was working on a group project and one of my group members was pretty disappointed because she found out she was not accepted to the summer medical program she applied to. I invited her to eat lunch with me one day and told her how much I admired her for her determination and dedication to her passions. I also made sure to let her know I appreciated her work on our project and thought her suggestions were great. After a few days, I noticed her attitude changed and she thanked me for being so considerate. That felt good."

This section is very insightful. Here Charlie reveals more personal aspects of his personality and preferences to try to demonstrate to the interviewer that he will be an asset to the company.

You'll also notice that Charlie has more difficulty with this line of questioning than the others and that is likely because motivation is an ability that has an ethereal quality to it. It's hard for a candidate to give a specific answer to what he or she finds motivational, so, now that you know it's a possible topic you'll have to talk about during an interview, you should prepare yourself by determining what you find motivational.

Although there is no harm in preparing yourself for an interview and thinking of answers to possible questions, make sure that your responses do not sound canned or coached. Always be leery of making generalizations and try to give detailed, specific examples of times when you actually demonstrated the skill.

INTERVIEWER: "Finally, I want to talk about stress management. Can you tell me what your current workplace is like in terms of stress and pressure?"

INTERVIEWEE: "Given that I'm just a volunteer, there isn't too much pressure placed on me. Sometimes, the office that we operate from can get hectic before one of our big events, but thankfully, we're usually pretty well prepared for those. Mostly, it's pretty casual and we all get along fairly well, so there's not a lot of stress. However, as the president of one of my school clubs, there can sometimes be a good deal of pressure on me. I want to make sure that everyone that attends the meetings feels involved, and picking out events for us to host at school can be stressful sometimes."

INTERVIEWER: "Can you tell me about a particularly stressful time that you encountered recently and how you handled it?"

INTERVIEWEE: "I actually mentioned this situation before, but it was when a donor called upset about the table she'd been placed at for one of our dinner events. She was really upset about what had happened, especially because she said she had specifically requested that she not be seated with the couple she was sitting next to. I wasn't in charge of making the table arrangements and didn't have the authority to change her seat so I tried to explain that to her. However, she was way too upset to listen to me, so she just ended up yelling when I told her I'd have to call her back about her problem. Although my supervisors were busy, I was able to get one to help me and she was able to take over the call and remedy the situation. Everything turned out OK, but it was the first time I'd ever had to deal with an upset donor of ours, so I was pretty anxious on the call."

INTERVIEWER: "Tell me about what triggers stress for you. Use a specific example."

INTERVIEWEE: "Well, that donor certainly stressed me out. I knew I was getting stressed because my heart started beating fast and I could feel my face turning red. I didn't want to upset the donor further, but I also didn't want her to keep yelling at me. Other times when I've been stressed I've started to shake and I could feel the adrenaline rushing inside me. Luckily, I'm an avid jogger so I can get all the tension out on a regular basis that way."

It was pretty obvious from the start of this topic that Charlie's ability to handle stress is not that great. However, it is also obvious that he has had little experience dealing with stress in the workplace, so it may be something that will diminish with time and experience.

INTERVIEWER: "Alright, well that's all we have for you. Thanks for coming in."

INTERVIEWEE: "Thank you. When should I expect to hear back from you?"

INTERVIEWER: "We will let you know within the next week."

INTERVIEWEE: "Sounds great. I look forward to it."

If you have any questions, and there wasn't a great time during the interview to ask them, be sure to ask them at the end. Here, Charlie asked when he would be hearing back from the interviewers. However, you can substitute any questions you may have.

Hopefully you found some examples in this interview that are helpful when you're reviewing the sample questions. You should expect your interview to be about 30 minutes or so. When you start applying for more professional jobs that require you to have, say, a college degree, they will spend more time interviewing you (perhaps an hour or more), and they are more likely to do multiple interviews.

While the situation may bring out anxiety in you, just remember that your future doesn't ride on this one interview. If it's your first one, go into it with the mindset that this is a practice round. You'll feel more at-ease, and you won't get your hopes up.

Whatever happens, just remember that you're confident, you're capable, and you're prepared (even if you don't feel like it).

In the next chapter, we'll talk about what you should be doing during the actual interview.

CHAPTER SIX

The Interview

You have a lot of information running through your brain right now; you may be wondering how there could be anything else on the subject.

Well, there's a lot. During the actual interview, you want to be your best self. We have lightly touched on some of these topics up to this point, but in this chapter, we will really dig into the following: composure, body language, tone of voice, eye contact, asking questions, and some general tips and tricks.

Composure

In really stressful times, the phrase "stay calm" or "be calm and composed" is often used. Being composed just means that you are calm, and you are in control of yourself.

When you're getting ready for the interview, you have to think about how you're going to come across, and composure is a huge part of that.

This is the last thing you want to have happen:

> Ten minutes late, you bust through the double doors. Your hair is frizzing pretty badly, the right side of your shirt is untucked, and you can see that you're wearing two different socks.

> You're out of breath. The receptionist can tell that you ran from the other side of the parking lot. There's a bead of sweat running down your spine and your armpits are really, and I mean *really*, wet.

> "Hi," you manage to say between heavy gulps of air, "I'm here," you breathe deeply, "for the interview."

> "You're late," the receptionist says, looking at you from under her tipped reading glasses.

> "Yeah, sorry about that," you say as you look down and quickly stuff the right side of your shirt in.

> "Have a seat," she motions.

> Your hands are shaking, and you sit down in the lobby. Your knees are shaking, too. There's air conditioning right above your head, but you still can't stop sweating. Your eyes are darting left and right, and you can't remember anything you studied for. Your stomach starts to feel really heavy and you realize you're panicking.

Hopefully you're laughing a little bit — this is not going to be you. Let's look at some things you can do to help you stay composed.

Answering questions

Don't know how to answer that question? No big deal. Ask the interviewer to repeat it. Still don't know how to answer? You have two options. Tell the interviewer that you just don't know. They'll move on, and it isn't the end of the world.

If you don't know how to answer the questions because it's a situation question, and you don't think you've been in that situation before, explain what you would do if you were in that situation.

In case that left you confused, here's an example: "Interviewer: Explain a situation where you helped an angry customer. You: Well, I've never been in a situation like that before, but if I were, I would…" Fill in the blank with what you would do. It answers the question effectively and you just dodged the dreaded "pass."

Be confident

I know, you're probably saying, "hey, you said that already!" You're right, but part of being composed is being sure of yourself.

Show a sense of natural confidence. No one is more confident in your abilities than you are. If you don't feel confident inside, act like you are anyway. You might be able to trick your brain into feeling more self-assured if you at least act like you are.

Calm your nerves

Go over the advice on calming your anxiety back in Chapter 2, and put it into practice. Chances are the interviewer is a bit nervous, too. Think of the interview as a conversation. Try to get to know the person as you might with the students in your class at the beginning of a new school year.

Body Language

The first impression you give will be a huge factor in determining whether or not you get the job. According to a study by Xerox, only 7 percent of all communication is verbal (qtd. in Stalter). That means that what you say isn't really that important — what you say with your tone of voice and body language is.

Here's an example: Your mom asks you to do the dishes after dinner. You look at her for a few seconds without saying anything. You sigh deeply and dramatically and say, "Okay," the pitch of your voice rising and falling. Your eyes are rolling and your hips have shifted.

Here's another example: Your mom asks you to do the dishes after dinner. Without moving, you quickly respond and say, "Okay," with a high, enthusiastic pitch to your voice. You smile and your posture is very upright.

In both instances above, the same words are used. However, you can see that the underlying body language determines how the communication is perceived.

Body language is a really detailed topic — you can read books upon books about the subject. However, let's just take a look at a few key concepts demonstrated in Harmony Stalter's book, *Employee Body Language Revealed*, that you can use when it comes to doing your first interview.

Smile, but not too much

Opening the interview with a smile is a great way to leave a positive first impression. However, don't smile more than the interviewer. If you smile too much or giggle a lot, you'll come across as silly or ditzy, which is unprofessional. This can also come across as a cover-up for your nervousness. Try to mirror what the interviewer is doing. When he or she smiles, smile back.

Nod your head

If you agree with something the interviewer is saying, nod your head. This is the universal, nonverbal sign for "I agree," which will let the interview know that you're listening to what they're saying.

Upright posture

Sit upright with your back straight. If you slouch, you won't look confident. With that being said, don't be stiff. If you sit still the whole time, it might freak out the interviewer. You're allowed to shift every once in a while; just don't let it take away from the interview.

Hands

Keeping your palms exposed gives off the sense that you are open and sincere. The best way to naturally have your palms exposed is to keep your hands in your lap, but have them facing up. You can let your right hand rest on your left hand, which feels natural, not forced.

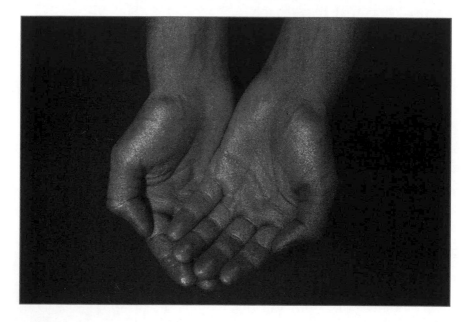

Also, don't touch your face, hair, or mouth. It looks fidgety, which is a sign of nervousness. You want the interviewer to know that you are prepared and confident.

Arms

Your arms are a huge part of body language reception. If you cross your arms, it can be an indication that you are being defensive. You might be showing that you are closed-minded. Avoid doing this during an interview.

If you have your arms behind your back, also known as hidden arms, you are sending a signal that you are hiding information or aren't being honest. Always keep your arms in sight; keeping your arms comfortably at your side is your best bet.

Fidgeting

When it comes to your feet and your hands, the most important thing to keep in mind is to avoid fidgeting. This is a sign of impatience and can make it seem like you want to run away. This might seem pretty accurate (can I run away now?), but avoid it. Focus on keeping your hands still and only shift positions every once in a while.

The handshake

The handshake is one of the most important parts of the interview process. For your first job interview, your employer might not be expecting a great handshake. However, if you deliver a professional, firm handshake, you're already exceeding expectations and are on your way to getting the job.

To have the perfect handshake, don't be too firm. It leaves the impression that you're overly aggressive. You'll know if it's too firm — this is the kind that actually hurts your hand.

On the other hand, don't be too shy. If you give a timid handshake that is limp, you'll send the signal that you're insecure.

Also, make sure your hands are dry. If you're nervous, you might get sweaty hands, which is unavoidable. However, avoid the wet handshake by rubbing your palms on your pants before you walk inside. Once you get the handshake out of the way, don't worry about your sweaty hands.

The best handshake is one that's firm, because "it conveys a sense of equality" (Stalter).

Practice your handshake with a friend or a parent. Get feedback on your grip — make sure you're being firm, because this is the best way to show right off the bat that you're confident.

Tone of voice

The pitch of your voice changes all the time depending on the context of what you're doing.

Think about going to a restaurant, for example. Have you ever noticed that your server greets you with a pretty high-pitched voice? — "Hey guys, how's it going?"

If your server is apologizing for something, you may notice that the pitch in his or her voice is a bit deeper — "I'm so sorry about that."

In general, a high-pitched voice is a sign of excitement, while a lower-pitched voice can be perceived as indicating anger. Now, in the example above, the server is trying to be empathetic. He or she is trying to show that they are angry *for* the customer, not *at* the customer.

Try not to be monotone, which means that you talk with the same tone of voice the entire time (think about how robots talk). This is a sign that you're bored.

Similar to fidgeting, talking fast can indicate that you're nervous. If you just talk normally, you'll send the signal that you're confident, which is what we want.

Eye contact

When you ask someone to give you their best advice when it comes to nailing an interview, one of the first things they'll probably tell you is to have great eye contact. The eyes are called "the window to the soul" for a reason. Where you look will send visual cues to the interviewer. Let's take a look at what each direction means.

Looking up

When you look up, it's a signal of recollection. You're thinking about a memory.

Looking down and to the left

This is a signal of contemplation. You're thinking about something pretty deeply.

Looking down and to the right

You're thinking about something emotional.

Looking straight down

This is the signal for shame or sympathy. If you're talking about empathy or sympathy during the interview, looking straight down will enhance your words.

Looking sideways

Try to avoid looking sideways. This is the signal for uncertainty, which will send the signal to the interviewer that you aren't 100 percent confident. If you notice that you're looking to the left or the right, stop doing it and look straight ahead.

In general, it is recommended that you hold eye contact for about 15 seconds at a time. Anything more makes you seem like you're trying to be intimidating and anything less makes you seem like you're not confident or that you're lying.

Looking into the eyes

If you look straight into the interviewers eyes, you are showing a sign of respect and attention. Eye contact also helps the other person feel more comfortable with you and is a sign of sincerity. You don't have to stare straight into their eyes the entire time, because this can feel unnatural, and it might actually freak out the interviewer. Be natural, but be aware that holding direct eye contact is the best way to appear confident and respectful.

To read more about eye contact, continue reading *Employee Body Language Revealed* by Harmony Stalter.

Don't overthink it

Knowing the basics of body language should help you, not hurt you. Don't go into the interview with all of these cues at the forefront of your mind. You want to be genuine, not fake.

The main idea here is to have a sense of what signals you're sending. If you notice that you're twirling your hair a lot, stop yourself, and put your hands comfortably on your lap. If you notice that you're talking really fast, slow down.

Finally, be aware that nonverbal communication is more believable than what you say. If your body language says that you're really nervous, but your words say that you're confident, the listener is more likely to listen to your body language.

Ask Questions

Don't forget the interview process can be a two-way street. When the formal interview is over, the interviewer might ask if you have any questions. This is a great time to show that you're really interested.

However, don't ask any questions that show that you're unprepared. You want the employer to know that you've done your homework. For example, don't ask what the hours of the store are — if you are interested in that, look at the website or even at the door to the building. You want to ask more specific questions that show your interest.

Here are some examples of some questions you can ask:

- How many people are employed here?
- Can you describe the work environment here?
- What would I be doing on a daily basis?
- What types of rules do you have that I may need to be aware of? (Perhaps target the question to a specific concern, such as dress code.)

- Is there anything else that you feel you want to go over?
- What types of advice would you give to someone in my position?
- When will a decision be made?

Even if you don't feel like asking a question, force yourself to ask at least one. The best question you can ask is when you will hear back — this gives you a timeline for when you should follow up. Your employer will be impressed, and you will be ending your interview with a good impression.

General Tips and Tricks

By now, you should be almost ready to master that interview. Here are some tips and tricks that you can use to make sure you get the job.

Don't chew gum

Sure, we all want fresh breath, but opt for brushing your teeth or having a mint. Chewing gum can leave a bad impression. According to a poll done by CareerBuilders, employers found that one of the most common mistakes that interviewees made was chewing gum, which was in the same list as answering a cellphone and appearing arrogant.

It's a simple thing to avoid, and it's one less thing to worry about when it comes to making a good impression.

Be early

The general rule of thumb that has been passed along through generations is: If you're early, you're on time. If you're on time, you're late. If you're late, don't bother showing up.

Show up to your interview five to 15 minutes early; if you have to wait, be patient. However, showing up early will show your employer that you're capable of being on time.

Use your best handwriting

If the application is a written one, focus on using your best handwriting. This is the first impression of all, and if you can leave a good one, you're on the road to success.

Find the space between humility and arrogance

Employers are turned off by arrogance, but being too humble can also turn them off. If you're too shy about your accomplishments, they won't get a sense of how great of a catch you are. Respectfully talk about what you're capable of without bragging.

Being arrogant: "Yeah, my dad owns a company, so I know how to do just about everything around here. He's taken me to some pretty fancy places, so let's just say I've been around the block."

Being confident: "I have a lot of experience working with people; I like to pay special attention to their body language and their tone of voice to completely understand how they feel about a particular service."

In the first example, the candidate is being arrogant by leaning on his dad to boost his ego as well as his "fancy" experiences. In the second example, the candidate is being confident by leaning on his own abilities.

CHAPTER SEVEN

Following Up

You nailed the interview, but you haven't heard back yet. In this chapter, we'll talk about when you should follow up (how soon is too soon?), how to do it (a phone call or a hand-written note?), and how often you should do it (I left 10 voicemails — did I go too far?).

When to Follow Up

Knowing when to follow up after an interview can be tough. You want to give the employer enough time to review your application and the interview, but you also want to make sure they know you are interested and are awaiting a response.

Employers can have very hectic schedules; sometimes, they need to be reminded to prioritize you — this is why following up is so important.

Hopefully at the end of the interview, you remembered to ask the question: "When should I expect to hear back from you?" or a variation of it. If the interviewer said something like "Expect to hear back from us in three days," wait three days.

There's no sense is following up after two days if the employer said he or she needs three. You run the risk of being pesky and making the wrong follow-up move.

If you were told it'd be a few days and it's day five or six, it's time to follow up.

If you forgot to ask that invaluable question at the end of the interview, the standard wait time is about a week. Force yourself to wait the seven days, and then continue on with your follow-up procedure.

How to Follow Up

So, it's been nine or 10 days and the employer said they'd get back to you within a week. It's time to follow up.

The best two ways to follow up are by phone or by email. If you do it by email, there's a little less pressure to perform in the moment. You can sit down and carefully craft your message, which should be laid-back in nature. Something along the lines of, "I'm just checking in to see where you are in the process" should work.

Make sure you aren't sending a paragraph — focus on keeping it short (about two or three lines). Oftentimes, employers are very busy and will either scan long emails or only read what's at the top.

If you follow up by phone, be polite and upbeat. You want to give the impression that you're patient, but interested. Say something like, "Hello, I was just calling to check in. How's the hiring process going? Is there anything else you need from me to help you make your decision?"

Another option that doesn't require any wait time at all is the thank you note. This a short note that you can send immediately following your interview. It can either be hand-written or emailed, and it should be a quick thank you to the interviewer for taking the time to talk to you. Make sure to use really good handwriting, though.

This is a great way to leave a lasting impression, and it might just be the cherry on top that gets you hired.

How Often to Follow Up

You waited the right amount of time and you emailed the employer. No response. What now?

First of all, don't put your job search on hold if you're waiting for a response. Keep your job hunt going and continue to do interviews at different places. Sometimes employers are so busy that they don't bother calling people back to tell them they aren't hired.

If you are being ignored, it's possible that the company isn't interested and either doesn't want to tell you — lame, right? — or they're too busy to make it a priority.

However, there is a chance that they either missed your email or didn't get a chance to respond. The average person gets hundreds of emails a day; it's very possible that your email either went to the junk folder or it just got lost in the clutter.

If you're following up a second time, wait another week. To recap: If the interview is on Monday, the general rule of thumb is to follow up the next Monday. No response? Follow up again the Monday after that.

If you are following up a second time, be overly polite and humble. Instead of saying, "I'm just checking in to see how things are going," switch to this: "Hello, I'm so sorry to disturb you; I know you are all very busy. I just wanted to send over a quick email to check back in on the process. Let me know if you need anything else from me."

If you send several follow ups and still aren't hearing back, it's worth directly asking if they want you to stop. "I know you are busy and understand that you may not have had time to reach out to me. However, if you want me to stop following up, just let me know. I don't want to send you emails if you aren't interested. Thanks again for you time."

In the words of Alexandra Franzen, communication expert, "Keep it short. Keep it simple. Keep it classy. Most importantly — Be unexpectedly generous" (**www.themuse.com**).

CHAPTER EIGHT

Starting Your Own Business

Starting a business is not for a select group of people, privileged individuals, or only adults. You do not have to come from a family who previously owned a business, and you definitely don't need to have a business degree — or any degree at all for that matter. Anyone who is motivated and passionate can run a business (I'm looking at you).

Why You Should (or Shouldn't)

Maybe you're furrowing your brows at the thought of starting your own business. Maybe you're smiling pretty intensely. Hopefully you're somewhere in the middle with a curious brow raise and a slight grin.

Before you get too excited, let's look at why you should (or shouldn't) start your own business.

Financial freedom

When you work for someone else, you get paid only for the time you actually work. When you work for yourself, you make money 24 hours a day, seven days a week, especially if you are selling on the Web.

You also get some tax breaks and benefits when you're doing your own thing, which is nice.

This also goes the other way, though. If you aren't successful, you aren't making money.

Flexible hours

When you work for yourself, you have the advantage of creating a schedule that can change as necessary so you can maintain your current school schedule. You can work more during breaks and take time off for exam week (not that you need it).

Your time, your training

When you work for yourself, you decide what is important for you to know. You will earn hands on training in a variety of subjects. In a corporate job, you would be limited to one job and one set of duties and responsibilities.

Responsibility

As your own boss, you are responsible for the successes or disappointments you face. As it stands right now, if you are working for someone else, you are giving that person full control over your situation.

By taking control of your future, you have no one to blame but yourself for your difficulties. On the other hand, you have no one to praise but yourself when you create a successful and marketable business.

Bragging rights

No, we didn't mean bragging to your classmates (although you could…), we meant bragging on your résumé! Being able to say that you started your own business is a great bullet point and conversation starter when it comes time to interview for that really scary job. It puts you one step ahead of everyone else.

Why other business fail, but you won't

One of the biggest reasons that small businesses fail is a bad business plan. Business plans are to a business owner like navigational systems are to a ship captain. It is the one thing that will keep you from crashing into business wasteland.

Here are some other reasons why business fail pretty quickly:

- Money runs out before the business can start making profits
- Bad managers
- Business owners get discouraged

- The health of the owners
- Obligations unforeseen by the owner

First of all, we're going to look at business options that aren't really going to cost you any money. Check.

Second of all, the kinds of businesses we have in mind don't require you to hire any managers. Check.

Third, you're young and youthful. Stay away from that sick kid, will you? Check.

You're starting on top. Let's take a look at some business ideas.

Business Options

So, you've decided you want to start your own business. That's great! That means you can skip the interview process (for now). Here are some ideas of possible businesses.

House sitting

When people go on vacation, what happens to their home? Are their personal belongings safe? You can make sure everything stays in place by offering house sitting services.

Your job would be to stay in the homes or to check in regularly and watch the personal belongings of families or individuals on vacation. You would be responsible for doing things like mowing the lawn, getting the mail, and keeping the home neat and tidy.

I know what you're thinking. How much money would I make? House sitters can make $200 to $500 per project, depending on the length and time the family needs your services. Many house sitters can make up to $20,000 annually.

This may sound like a great idea in theory, but it is realistic. To get started, talk to homeowners that you know and those in your area. Put up fliers in community centers offering your service.

If this still doesn't sound like something you could do, look at the site **www.housecarers.com** to read some house sitting articles.

Pet sitting

Houses not really your thing? What about animals? Professional pet sitting is more than just a walk-your-dog-for-an-hour business. This is like babysitting, but with an animal. The profession has grown into the thousands, due largely in part to the number of households and families getting family pets.

If you decide this sounds like fun, these are some of things you'd be doing:

- Walking the animals on a regular basis
- Keeping them while the family is away
- Taking them to vet appointments
- Visiting them

You don't need a master's degree or anything to do this job, but you do need to love animals and have some kind of knowledge about animal behavior and health. If this is something you're interested, read some books on the subject.

Here are some recommendations:

- *How to Listen to Your Cat: The Complete Guide to Communicating with Your Feline Friend* by Kim O. Morgan
- *How to Listen to Your Dog: The Complete Guide to Communicating with Man's Best Friend* by Carlotta Cooper
- *How to Housetrain Your Puppy in 14 Days or Less: The Complete Guide to Training Your Dog* by Gretchen Pearson, DVM
- *How To Open & Operate a Financially Successful Pet Sitting Business* by Angela William Duea

Pet sitters can make anywhere from $20,000 to $40,000 annually, depending on how many pets they care for in a week. You may be paid on an hourly basis or per project. Negotiate — this is your business after all.

Don't know where to start? Contact local shelters to offer your services to animals without owners. Contact veterinarians, pet stores, animal hospitals, pet groomers, and animal boarding houses to offer affiliate services with them.

Still not sure if it's for you? Visit the following websites and take a look around: **www.petsit.com** and **www.petsitters.org**.

Tutoring

If you're really good at a subject, you're probably used to your friends asking you for help (what's the answer to question 3 again?). Why not get paid for it?

Tutors work one-on-one with students and individuals in a range of areas. You can be a tutor that will help with all areas or you can be a specialty tutor of one of the following subjects:

- Reading
- Math
- English
- Computers
- Science
- History
- Government
- College Prep

"Patience is a virtue" is not just a saying with this line or work. You need to have patience of steel to work as a tutor. You also have to be good at communicating.

For personal instruction, you can charge whatever you want, the standard being from $30 to $125 per hour, or you can charge a per project fee (per project meaning until the person you're working with understands the material). Annually, tutors can make anywhere from $20,000 to $75,000.

To get started, contact schools and other vocational institutes to offer your services to children or adults in their organizations. You can let the office staff at your school know that you're interested in tutoring, and to give you some credibility, you can ask your teachers to write you a letter of recommendation. This will let the parents know that you're actually good at the subject you want to teach.

If you want to learn a little bit more about tutoring, visit **www.american tutoringassociation.org** and **www.reading-tutors.com.**

You can also read the book *The Teen's Ultimate Guide to Making Money When You Can't Get a Job* by Julie Fryer, which has an entire chapter on tutoring.

Lawn care

Can't get enough of the outdoors? Lawn care might be for you.

The basics of lawn care include mowing grass, trimming bushes, weed eating, and taking care of grass clippings and leaves.

The best way to figure out how much to charge for your lawn care business is up to you. However, a proven model when you first start out is to ask your client to set the price. Once you establish yourself, you can start charging a fixed price. A generally accepted fixed price that is competitive, but will still make you money is $35-$45 per half acre and $25-$30 for a small lawn.

To get started, you can go door-to-door and say something along the lines of, "Hi, I've been wanting to make a little money this summer. If you need help taking care of your lawn, I'm your guy/girl."

Word-of-mouth and social media are also going to help you find customers.

To read more on the subject, visit **www.postandcourier.com/article/20120603/pc1207/120609873** to read an article about Billy's lawn care success story.

Growing and selling produce

Now, this sounds like a stretch, but it isn't impossible. If you live in a climate where you can grow produce, there are people who want to buy it. Think of it as your own personal farmers market.

The best way to sell produce like this is to go around the neighborhood and — you guessed it — go door-to-door.

You can sell fresh produce for comparable prices to the grocery store and in some cases, maybe even a little more. In this case, how much you make will depend on how much you produce.

It doesn't cost a lot to start a small garden, and you may even find that it becomes a passion.

To learn how to grow fresh fruits and vegetables, read the Back to Basics series on how to grow fresh plants. Some of these books include:

- *How to Build, Maintain, and Use a Compost System: Secrets and Techniques You Need to Know to Grow the Best Vegetables* by Kelly Smith
- *How to Grow Fruits, Vegetables & Houseplants Without Soil: The Secrets of Hydroponic Gardening Revealed* by Rick Helweg
- *The Complete Guide to Growing Tomatoes: A Complete Step-by-Step Guide Including Heirloom Tomatoes* by Cherie Everhart

Getting Started

If you have decided that one of these business options sounds like something you can do (or if you have an idea of your own), you need to test out your concept. Your family and friends can offer great insight into whether your business idea will work. Knowing them on a personal level will make it easier for you to explain your concept and how you plan to make your business idea happen. They may even have some suggestions on how to make it better or where to look for some customers.

When you do address your family and friends, you want to be in a casual setting. Ask them about the business as you would ask how your outfit looks, subtle but serious. Here are some questions you should think about asking:

- How much will the public like/need my product or service?
- Who would most use/buy my product or service?
- How much would individuals be willing to spend on my product or service?
- How often will my product or service be in demand?

- How can I make this a product or service my customers will need many times throughout the year?
- Which income bracket are my clients in?

When you finish asking questions and feel confident that you're ready to get started, you need to create a business plan.

Creating a Business Plan

Creating a business plan doesn't have to be complicated — especially if you're running a one-man (or woman) show. After all, you're not trying to build a corporation here; you're trying to make a little extra cash.

Making a business plan may seem a little "extra" if you know what I mean, but it's great practice for the future, and it gives you a clear direction. When you're asked about your business in the future, say during that coveted interview, how cool would it be if you whipped out a business plan?

The basics of a professional business plan include the following parts (all concepts here taken from the U.S. Small Business Administration website at **www.sba.gov**):

- Executive Summary: This is a snapshot of your business idea. In this section, you want to talk about your goals.
- Company Description: This is where you walk about what you're doing (the service you're providing or the product you're producing). What makes your business different from all the others and what market are you serving?

- Market Analysis: In this section, you want to take a look at your competition and compare yourself to them. For example, if you decide to start a lawn care business, ask around and find out what people are doing right now for lawn care. If they're using a company in town that's known for doing lawn care, find out what they're charging and put that information here.
- Organization & Management: This has to do with the structure of your business. Unless you plan on having a full-fledged staff, you can probably skip this part.
- Service or Product Line: This is where you tell the story of your product or service. What are you selling, how is it helping other people, and what is the product's life cycle?
- Marketing & Sales: If you plan on putting up fliers or using social media, put that here. Your sales strategy lives here.
- Funding Request: This section is used for businesses that don't have enough money to start. You won't need to use this section.
- Financial Projections: This is kind of connected to the funding request. If you are going to have to ask for money, this gives the lenders an idea of how much you expect to make. It's good practice to go ahead and include this, though. How much are hoping to make?
- Appendix: While this is optional, if you want to include it, you can. You put your résumé back here as well as any other "logistical" information you may have.

Don't be scared of the business plan. If you do make one, it can be a great way to give you and your business some credibility. Trying to get a new customer? Show them that business plan so that they know you're serious.

CHAPTER NINE

Job Logistics

Wow, you're almost to the end of the book. By now, you're an expert on all things "business," right? You know how to get a job, how to nail that interview, and even how to start your own business.

It's all fun and games until the paperwork shows up to play. Paperwork can be confusing and foreign, so in this last chapter, you're going to learn how to handle taxes (ew), how to fill out an application (less ew?), and how to create a résumé (maybe not so bad?).

Tax Information

When you land that job, you'll notice that your paychecks are not quite as much as you thought they might be. (I make 8.25 an hour, and I worked 20 hours; why is my paycheck less than $165?) That's the taxman.

Depending on what state you live in, you may or may not have to pay state income tax, but no matter where you go, you're going to have to pay federal taxes.

The government needs information from you in order to make sure they're taxing you right. When you get the job, you're going to see a form that looks like this:

Form W-4 (2016)

Purpose. Complete Form W-4 so that your employer can withhold the correct federal income tax from your pay. Consider completing a new Form W-4 each year and when your personal or financial situation changes.

Exemption from withholding. If you are exempt, complete only lines 1, 2, 3, 4, and 7 and sign the form to validate it. Your exemption for 2016 expires February 15, 2017. See Pub. 505, Tax Withholding and Estimated Tax.

Note: If another person can claim you as a dependent on his or her tax return, you cannot claim exemption from withholding if your income exceeds $1,050 and includes more than $350 of unearned income (for example, interest and dividends).

Exceptions. An employee may be able to claim exemption from withholding even if the employee is a dependent, if the employee:
- Is age 65 or older,
- Is blind, or
- Will claim adjustments to income; tax credits; or itemized deductions, on his or her tax return.

The exceptions do not apply to supplemental wages greater than $1,000,000.

Basic instructions. If you are not exempt, complete the **Personal Allowances Worksheet** below. The worksheets on page 2 further adjust your withholding allowances based on itemized deductions, certain credits, adjustments to income, or two-earners/multiple jobs situations.

Complete all worksheets that apply. However, you may claim fewer (or zero) allowances. For regular wages, withholding must be based on allowances you claimed and may not be a flat amount or percentage of wages.

Head of household. Generally, you can claim head of household filing status on your tax return only if you are unmarried and pay more than 50% of the costs of keeping up a home for yourself and your dependent(s) or other qualifying individuals. See Pub. 501, Exemptions, Standard Deduction, and Filing Information, for information.

Tax credits. You can take projected tax credits into account in figuring your allowable number of withholding allowances. Credits for child or dependent care expenses and the child tax credit may be claimed using the **Personal Allowances Worksheet** below. See Pub. 505 for information on converting your other credits into withholding allowances.

Nonwage income. If you have a large amount of nonwage income, such as interest or dividends, consider making estimated tax payments using Form 1040-ES, Estimated Tax for Individuals. Otherwise, you may owe additional tax. If you have pension or annuity income, see Pub. 505 to find out if you should adjust your withholding on Form W-4 or W-4P.

Two earners or multiple jobs. If you have a working spouse or more than one job, figure the total number of allowances you are entitled to claim on all jobs using worksheets from only one Form W-4. Your withholding usually will be most accurate when all allowances are claimed on the Form W-4 for the highest paying job and zero allowances are claimed on the others. See Pub. 505 for details.

Nonresident alien. If you are a nonresident alien, see Notice 1392, Supplemental Form W-4 Instructions for Nonresident Aliens, before completing this form.

Check your withholding. After your Form W-4 takes effect, use Pub. 505 to see how the amount you are having withheld compares to your projected total tax for 2016. See Pub. 505, especially if your earnings exceed $130,000 (Single) or $180,000 (Married).

Future developments. Information about any future developments affecting Form W-4 (such as legislation enacted after we release it) will be posted at www.irs.gov/w4.

Personal Allowances Worksheet (Keep for your records.)

A   Enter "1" for **yourself** if no one else can claim you as a dependent . . . . A ____

B   Enter "1" if:
- You are single and have only one job; or
- You are married, have only one job, and your spouse does not work; or
- Your wages from a second job or your spouse's wages (or the total of both) are $1,500 or less.

  . . . B ____

C   Enter "1" for your **spouse**. But, you may choose to enter "-0-" if you are married and have either a working spouse or more than one job. (Entering "-0-" may help you avoid having too little tax withheld.) . . . . C ____

D   Enter number of **dependents** (other than your spouse or yourself) you will claim on your tax return . . . . . . D ____

E   Enter "1" if you will file as **head of household** on your tax return (see conditions under **Head of household** above) . . . E ____

F   Enter "1" if you have at least $2,000 of **child or dependent care expenses** for which you plan to claim a credit . . . F ____
    (**Note: Do not** include child support payments. See Pub. 503, Child and Dependent Care Expenses, for details.)

G   **Child Tax Credit** (including additional child tax credit). See Pub. 972, Child Tax Credit, for more information.
- If your total income will be less than $70,000 ($100,000 if married), enter "2" for each eligible child; then **less** "1" if you have two to four eligible children or **less** "2" if you have five or more eligible children.
- If your total income will be between $70,000 and $84,000 ($100,000 and $119,000 if married), enter "1" for each eligible child . . G ____

H   Add lines A through G and enter total here. (**Note:** This may be different from the number of exemptions you claim on your tax return.) ▶ H ____

For accuracy, complete all worksheets that apply.
- If you plan to **itemize** or claim **adjustments to income** and want to reduce your withholding, see the **Deductions and Adjustments Worksheet** on page 2.
- If you are **single** and have **more than one job** or are **married** and you **and your spouse both work** and the combined earnings from all jobs exceed $50,000 ($20,000 if married), see the **Two-Earners/Multiple Jobs Worksheet** on page 2 to avoid having too little tax withheld.
- If **neither** of the above situations applies, **stop here** and enter the number from line H on line 5 of Form W-4 below.

- - - - - - - - - - Separate here and give Form W-4 to your employer. Keep the top part for your records. - - - - - - - - - -

Form W-4 — Employee's Withholding Allowance Certificate

Department of the Treasury
Internal Revenue Service

▶ Whether you are entitled to claim a certain number of allowances or exemption from withholding is subject to review by the IRS. Your employer may be required to send a copy of this form to the IRS.

OMB No. 1545-0074

2016

1 Your first name and middle initial	Last name		2 Your social security number

Home address (number and street or rural route)	3 ☐ Single ☐ Married ☐ Married, but withhold at higher Single rate.
	Note: If married, but legally separated, or spouse is a nonresident alien, check the "Single" box.
City or town, state, and ZIP code	4 If your last name differs from that shown on your social security card, check here. You must call 1-800-772-1213 for a replacement card. ▶ ☐

5   Total number of allowances you are claiming (from line H above **or** from the applicable worksheet on page 2)   5 ____

6   Additional amount, if any, you want withheld from each paycheck . . . . 6 $ ____

7   I claim exemption from withholding for 2016, and I certify that I meet **both** of the following conditions for exemption.
- Last year I had a right to a refund of **all** federal income tax withheld because I had **no** tax liability, **and**
- This year I expect a refund of **all** federal income tax withheld because I expect to have **no** tax liability.
If you meet both conditions, write "Exempt" here . . . . ▶ 7 ____

Under penalties of perjury, I declare that I have examined this certificate and, to the best of my knowledge and belief, it is true, correct, and complete.

Employee's signature
(This form is not valid unless you sign it.) ▶   Date ▶

8 Employer's name and address (Employer: Complete lines 8 and 10 only if sending to the IRS.)	9 Office code (optional)	10 Employer identification number (EIN)

For Privacy Act and Paperwork Reduction Act Notice, see page 2.   Cat. No. 10220Q   Form **W-4** (2016)

This worksheet can look really complicated, but here are the basic steps to getting it done.

If you live with your parents, you are considered "dependent." In that case, you enter "0" on line "A." If you only have one job, you can enter "1" on line "B." Leave lines C-G blank. On line, H, you enter the total of all the numbers you've written down, which will probably be "1."

The rest of the form is super simple. Just put in your name, your social security number (SSN), your address, and the fact that you're single. In line 5, you just copy the number that's in line H above, which was most likely "1." If you decide you want your employer to take out more money, you can fill in box 6, but that is optional. You're done!

Quick note: Your social security number should be extremely private. This is the information hackers use to commit identity fraud which could ruin your life.

Don't freak out. Just make sure you either memorize your SSN or keep it in a safe place to refer to it. Don't keep it in your wallet or purse — there is a chance you could lose it.

Filling Out an Application

Nowadays, a lot of job applications are online. However, there are a significant amount of employers that still do paper applications. Below is the first page of what a paper application will look like.

Sample Employment Application Form

PLEASE PRINT ALL INFORMATION REQUESTED EXCEPT SIGNATURE	

APPLICATION FOR EMPLOYMENT

APPLICANTS MAY BE TESTED FOR ILLEGAL DRUGS

PLEASE COMPLETE PAGES 1-4.   DATE _____

Name _____
       Last   First   Middle   Maiden

Present address _____
       Number   Street   City   State   Zip

How long _____   Social Security No. _____ – ____ – _____

Telephone ( )_____

If under 18, please list age _____

                                        Days/hours available to work
Position applied for (1) _____   No Pref _____   Thur _____
and salary desired   (2) _____   Mon _____   Fri _____
(Be specific)   Tue _____   Sat _____
                                           Wed _____   Sun _____

How many hours can you work weekly? _____   Can you work nights? _____

Employment desired   __ FULL-TIME ONLY   __ PART-TIME ONLY   __ FULL- OR PART-TIME

When available for work?_____

TYPE OF SCHOOL	NAME OF SCHOOL	LOCATION (Complete mailing address)	NUMBER OF YEARS COMPLETED	MAJOR & DEGREE
High School				
College				
Bus. or Trade School				
Professional School				

HAVE YOU EVER BEEN CONVICTED OF A CRIME?   __ No   __ Yes

If yes, explain number of conviction(s), nature of offense(s) leading to conviction(s), how recently such offense(s) was/were committed, sentence(s) imposed, and type(s) of rehabilitation. _____

This is the general idea of a paper application. Usually, there will be a backside that asks you to list references. These are people that you are not related to that can vouch for you being a good worker. Examples of good references include past employers, your pastor, and teachers.

Many applications will also require you to give your social security number (SSN).

Creating a Résumé (Optional)

Although most positions that you will be applying to will not require a résumé, creating one to give to a hiring manager is an easy way to set you apart from the competition.

A résumé is a communication tool that highlights what you can bring to the table. It shows what you have to offer.

If you decide that you want to create a résumé, some things you would want to include are:

- Your grades/GPA
- Any clubs or organizations you are involved with (the chess club, national honors society)
- Any class positions you have had (secretary, vice president)
- Volunteer work
- Your education history

At the top of the page, you need to have your full name. Include your full address and phone number. Put down your main email address where you can be contacted. Make sure the email address is a professional sounding one. Just because we can have cute or unique email addresses does not mean they are the best idea for a résumé (hotbabe23?).

You'll also want to include some references (names, addresses, phone number, email address, and how you know them). This is the same kind of information that you may be asked to include on your actual application.

Only list people who are going to give you a positive reference or those who know you well enough to answer questions about you. This person can make or break your ability to get this job.

Contact the people you're listing and confirm that they agree to be your reference. It's standard politeness code.

You can create your resume on your computer either from scratch or from a template. It's really important that you have someone look over your résumé, both for content and for mistakes. The last thing you want is to have some silly grammar mistake in there.

Make sure you're organized to show how great an employee you would be!

CONCLUSION

You're ready to take the job market by storm. You have all the tools you need to blow your future employer away.

The most important thing of all is to be yourself. Yes, there are tools you can use to help you leave a great first impression, but the idea is that you are showcasing your best self, not a different person.

Your employer wants to get to know you, so be honest and put your best foot forward.

You have what it takes — now go land that job!

REFERENCES

Chansky, Tamar E. "Overcoming Job Interview Anxiety: How to Be Calm, Cool and Confident." Worry Wise, 27 Mar. 2013. Web. 25 Feb. 2016.

Franzen, Alexandra. "Emails That Land Jobs: The Best Way to Shine in a Follow-Up Note." Daily Muse, Inc. Web. 25 Feb. 2016.

Fryer, Julie. *The Teen's Ultimate Guide to Making Money When You Can't Get a Job: 199 Ideas for Earning Cash on Your Own Terms*. Ocala, FL: Atlantic Pub. Group, 2012. Print.

Harris Interactive. "Employers Reveal Outrageous and Common Mistakes Candidates Made in Job Interviews." CareerBuilder, 12 Jan. 2011. Web. 25 Feb. 2016.

Lewis, Chris. "High Anxiety: Three Simple Ways to Calm Your Nerves." *Maria Droste Counseling Center*. Maria Droste, 10 June 2013. Web. 25 Feb. 2016.

Onion, Amanda. "Psychologists Say 'Um' and 'Uh' Have Meaning." ABC News Network. Web. 25 Feb. 2016.

Stalter, Harmony. *Employee Body Language Revealed: How to Predict Behavior in the Workplace by Reading and Understanding Body Language.* Ocala, FL: Atlantic Pub. Group, 2011. Print.

U.S. Small Business Administration. "How to Write a Business Plan." Web. 25 Feb. 2016.

United States Department of Labor. Web. 25 Feb. 2016.

Withers, Robert. "80% - The Key to Your Job Search." *ProMatch.* ProMatch, 18 June 2014. Web. 25 Feb. 2016.

YouthRules! Web. 25 Feb. 2016.

GLOSSARY

COMPOSURE   The state or feeling of being calm and in control of oneself.

ELOQUENT   Fluent or persuasive in speaking or writing.

EMPATHY   The ability to understand and share the feelings of another.

ETHICS   A system of moral principles.

ETHOS   An appeal to ethics; a means of convincing someone of the character or credibility of the persuader.

INTERPERSONAL   Relationships or communication between people.

JOB APPLICATION   A paper form that requires you to fill out many questions. It is often a duplicate of your résumé, but still needs to be filled out carefully, honestly, and clearly.

JOB BOARD   These are sometimes called job sites. There are several different types of job boards like general, industry specific, geographic, niche specific, and company centers.

JOB INTERVIEW   This is a meeting between a job candidate and an interviewer looking to hire the right person. Questions are asked about experience, accomplishments, and skills to determine whether the applicant is a good match.

JOB SKILLS   The skills you need to do a particular job. For example, an accountant needs to have good math and accounting skills; a doctor needs to have good medical, scientific, and personal skills.

LETTER OF RECOMMENDATION   A letter that is written to support your skills, ability, and work ethic, usually written when applying to graduate school.

NETWORKING   Interacting with other people to exchange information and develop contacts, especially to further one's career.

PHONE INTERVIEW   This is when a job interview is conducted via telephone.

POLITICALLY CORRECT   A term primarily used to describe language, policies, or measures which are intended not to offend or disadvantage any particular group of people in society.

REFERENCE LIST   This is the list of people whom a prospective employer can contact for references.

REFERENCES   These are people who know you and will say good things about you. They could be coworkers, educational references, or personal references.

REFERRAL LETTER   A type of cover letter that uses name-dropping to attract the reader and get an interview.

RÉSUMÉ   A key job-hunting tool used to get an interview; it summarizes your accomplishments, education, and work experience, and should reflect your special mix of skills and strengths.

SHORT-LISTED   A list of preferable items or candidates that have been selected for final consideration, as in making an award or filling a position.

TACT   Sensitivity in dealing with others or with difficult issues.

THANK YOU LETTER   After every interview, you should send a thank you letter to each person who interviewed you.

UNDERQUALIFIED   This is when you do not have the required qualifications for a position.

INDEX